9 DARING STORIES OF COURAGE

Introduced by **Debora Luzi**

WOMEN WHO

Dare TO

Desire

A journey to remember who you are

'*Women Who Dare to Desire* is a truly beautiful and inspiring book. There is something really special about a group of women coming together in this way and sharing their unique stories and perspectives.

With each story you feel as though you are being taken on a journey through the writer's transformation for yourself, and the exercises at the end of each chapter help you to integrate everything.

The women's stories in this book will change you. They will cause you to question things, to think differently, to shift your mindset. These women will inspire, motivate and educate you and will leave you with the deep knowing that you too can be a woman who dares to desire.'

Dina Behrman, PR Strategist & Publisher

'I so so so LOVE the concept of this book. I have seen many books and authored a few myself, but this book not only shares inspirational stories, it also guides you through transformations illustrating real examples and provides additional downloadable resources, space for reflections and 'hands-on exercises'.

Beautifully put together - by the way, when you get to the end, there is a BIG surprise – a MUST read!!!'

Sabine Matharu, Business Growth Strategist

'I loved these stories of women unabashedly owning their desire, creativity, vulnerability, and power. With space for your own reflections, insights, and healing after each chapter, this book will wake you up, shake you up, and lift you up in the juiciest way!'

Leza Lowitz, internationally acclaimed yoga and mindfulness teacher and best-selling author of over 20 books

'I've read numerous anthology books written to inspire the reader but this is the first collection of stories that have offered a glimpse behind the velvet curtain of the process each woman has taken to achieve her desires and help others to do the same.

The stories are inspiring and insightful. I felt like I had come the closest I could come to walking a few steps in the shoes of each woman.

The exercises are simple powerfully effective. Each one offers a unique opportunity to explore self, whilst removing a layer of shoulds to uncover ones deepest desires.

Tina's grow and reflect exercise is a brilliant reminder of how to reconnect with one's body in all its glory through touch.

Deborah's desire to birth a book where we as readers can journey with the author has been realised and captures the zeitgeist of the intersection of femininity and spirituality of 2023 perfectly.

This book will change your life.'

Brenda Gabriel, Fame PR Queen

Published by Goldcrest Books International Ltd
www.goldcrestbooks.com
publish@goldcrestbooks.com

ISBN: 978-1-913719-87-6

To my mother, Florise, to my grandmothers, Lina, Adriana and Elena, to my great-grandmothers and to my great-great-grandmothers who made my existence possible. To their buried desires. This book is for them and for any woman who has had to put herself last because she did not have freedom of speech and expression.

We are here to give them a voice and tell them they are perfect just as they are.

I, ...KATY YASINSAC......

AM A WOMAN WHO
DARES TO DESIRE.

And SO IT IS!

Let's start by declaring to yourself and the world that you are a woman who dares to desire. Add your name, your fingerprint and the mark of your lips on this page.

"'In the evening of life, we will be judged on love alone' said St. John's of the Cross. Every woman is called to leave a footprint in the world, a legacy that will live after she has gone. Being sure that love is made tangible by our actions, we share with you our stories as small gifts of love. Stories of growth, redemption, awareness. Stories of love for our purpose, message, and ultimate desire."

Elisa Colangeli

"Immortal" by Elisa Colangeli

Being a woman who dares to desire is a blessing and a misfortune at the same time.

We are women who stand in our power,

Who go against the current,

Against what society expects of us.

We are women rising,

Feeling our potency,

Our desires.

We are the women who are ready to rewrite history,

The stories of how a woman should behave and exist.

We hold the suppressed power of our grandmothers and great-great-grandmothers.

We are not women who watch the stars

And wish to be amongst them,

We are women who desire to be the stars

Shining in all their beauty,

In the sadness of the conflicts

And in the duality of who we are.

We are ready to shed tears for the things we lose

And embrace the happiness of the things we gain and ...

The happiness of the woman we are ready to become.

Debora Luzi
Founder of *Women Who Dare to Desire*

Contents

PREFACE

"Desire" was the first word whispered at me.

Years ago, when I started my healing journey, I created a beautiful group called Empower Your Life Now.

I had empowered myself so much after many life challenges that I now wanted to share my empowerment with others.

However, something did not feel right with the name and its meaning.

I thought there was more behind my mission and intention.

So I asked my intuition to guide me to the right name. For a while I carried a small notebook with me wherever I went, hoping that intuition would speak. But nothing. I knew I had to be patient and fully trust.

One night I found myself attending an interesting workshop in London. One of the facilitators gave us a brick and asked us to write a word on it and stick it in a pile with all the others.

To my surprise, the first word that came to my mind was "desire".

The first thought that then came to my mind was, "Do I have unfinished business with desire?"

I stopped questioning, got out of my logical mind and wrote the word on the brick.

Desire ... I felt as if I had the first piece of the puzzle for my new group and movement.

I did not have to wait much longer for more whispers to show up and deliver the rest.

A few nights later, I could not sleep. The word desire was constantly in my mind. I was thinking about my own desires. The one I had the courage to meet in person and the one whom I had never met.

With an exhausted brain after so much thinking, I managed to fall asleep until ...

It was 2 a.m. when a voice, a whisper, suddenly woke me up.

I was sweating, my heart was beating fast ...

"Dare," said the voice, "Dare" "Dare"... "Dare, Debora"... "Dare to desire woman, for you, and any woman who is ready to listen to their call, and light the fire in their heart."

I switched on the light and wrote down the words you have seen on the front cover of this book: "Women Who Dare to Desire".

BOOM! I had it.

A movement had begun on that very night.

A movement that would inspire all the women on the planet to dare more, to go for what they truly love and desire, without ifs or buts.

A movement that would allow women to be (too much), to own their voice, their greatness, their light, without any justifications.

In January 2020, just before the global lockdown, the Women Who Dare to Desire Conference took the stage in London, showcasing 18 inspiring speakers who had stories to share to empower other women.

I created the conference as a result of my own struggle to speak on stage, because I did not have enough following at the time, and because I did not have a TEDX talk on my achievement box.

The ethos of the movement gave me the strength to move forward, to dare to follow my passion, despite the naysayers, the fears of my own mind and despite what I was supposed to be and do, according to the industry's eye.

Around November 2021 the idea for this book came to mind. I was resisting it so much as I did not want it to be another anthology of stories, I wanted it to be a book where the readers could go on a journey with the authors and write their own powerful stories.

I started to look for nine powerful women who had a desire to become an author, but who had not given life to this desire yet.

Their desire was looking for me, and I was looking for them.

So here we are, writing this book for you with the hope that it will awaken something in you that you might have forgotten, something that is dormant in you and that is just waiting to be awakened, nurtured, shared and most of all LIVED ... against all odds ...

Because ...

WE ARE WOMEN WHO DARE TO DESIRE

With much daring love,

Debora Luzi

HOW TO ENJOY WOMEN
WHO DARE TO DESIRE

When I had the idea for this book, I wanted to create something that the reader could deeply feel and experience.

I did not want our authors to just share a story, I wanted them to give you a ticket for the ride they went on.

I wanted the reader to shift and change with each author, to go deep within themselves and experience the transformations that each author experienced.

Each author has written a beautiful and inspiring story of how they have dared to desire and follow their dreams and their passion.

After the story, each author will invite you on to a unique journey. They will give you some ideas, reflections and actions to take so that you can embark on your own transformation and quest for the message hidden between the lines, the one you might be waiting for.

Remain open and curious. Do NOT stop at the surface; go a little bit deeper within yourself each time and see what you can find that you might have forgotten.

I am a firm believer that owning our voice and who we are is one of the most important things we can do in our life and business.

Giving women permission to speak their voices is my ultimate mission.

I want women to feel free to express themselves. I do not want to give them templates or rules, I want their words to come from their heart, with no restrictions, no boundaries ... with pure, utter freedom.

For this reason, you will find many different tones of voice in this book and different styles of writing and expression. I did not want the authors to filter who they are to fit in this book, I wanted them to create the tone for this book with who they are.

You will find more conversational stories, others with more of a storytelling style and others more direct.

This is the beauty of this book, which we hope you will appreciate.

Our motto is "Write with freedom from the heart, whatever that might look like. Write as if no one is watching."

I still remember when I wrote my first e-book and gave it to my two teacher friends to proofread. They gave me the manuscript back with all the spelling mistakes highlighted and they added this note: "You wrote the book in a very conversational way using everything we do not teach at school when it comes to writing novels or essays."

For a moment I froze. I wanted to rip all the pages off and forget about the idea of publishing the book.

I stayed with the discomfort and doubt for a few days until I realised that I could not have it any other way. This is HOW I WRITE, this is WHO I AM, and I love it. This is what I teach women, to be 100% who they truly are with no filters and rules, so I decided to lead by example again because I am a WOMAN WHO DARES TO DESIRE.

Each author has created their own way to communicate and connect with you, either via written prompts, exercises, or drawing. I am sure you will enjoy these different styles and journeys.

In the end, we want you to stop and reflect and make a conscious decision on all the things you have learnt and discovered about yourself.

The final cherry on the cake will be our invitation to you to write your own story.

We invite you to write it and share it in any way you like.

Maybe your own book will be born after reading this, maybe you will want to travel the world and start to share your story on stage, or maybe you will want to create your own events and groups to allow other people to share their stories and get inspired.

The WORD will be your OYSTER at the end.

I know you know what to do with it.

Remember, the sky is the limit!

May this book be the catalyst to help you remember who you are and what you came here to do.

I am a woman who gives a physical tangible dimension to emotions that otherwise you wouldn't dare to name.

ELISA COLANGELI

Elisa is a figurative artist, who mainly portrays women. She has developed her original and insightful approach to female portraiture based on the study of archetypes, and her emotional, dreamlike paintings represent a tribute to the beauty of the soul.

Her art is sold all over the world and she teaches art classes online. She is the founder of the 'BeART! Hub', a free Facebook community where she encourages members to nurture their creative side through the practice of art and, by unlocking possible creative paths for business, self-development or leisure time, live a fulfilling and colourful life.

Elisa is mother of two boys, a full-time environmental engineer and a cat-lover.

Elisa's Secrets

I spent part of my honeymoon on the Santiago walk in Spain, where my husband and I walked 320 km in 14 days.

I did parasailing in Mexico, flying suspended in the air above the ocean – and sharks!

When I was a child, I used to hate my curly hair and once I tried to cut it to make some adjustments, but afterwards I was almost bald!

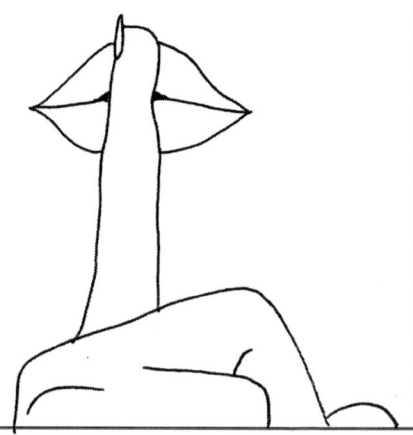

Call me by my name

I lived in a fragile soap bubble. I was a kid who was afraid of other kids. I could see the world, but I could not experience it fully, as I was always ill. I missed real gaming buddies, skirmishes and getting dirty during lunchtime at the kindergarten. I did not even know the difference between a pen and a pencil when I began primary school. My mates could write words and numbers, but I was silent and felt the heaviness of my first time in real life.

Then the bubble popped.

A Sunday afternoon, three decades later, and after a juicy lasagne, an espresso and some chats, I noticed that my friend Cristina had brought with her some oil paints and a painting.

"I want to show you what I am learning at the art school, we are copying some paintings by Van Gogh."

Looking at her reproduction, I could recognize an attempt at the typical brush strokes of impressionism mixed with the diligence of a scholar.

Undoubtedly, her eyes were radiant with joy and satisfaction for the results displayed.

She used to call colors by specific names. A yellow was not just a yellow, but a cadmium or an ochre, a specific blue was different from another blue. You can't compare the greyish blue darkness of a stormy sea to the brightness of a Mexican turquoise stone, therefore many names for many colors. I felt lost in that new vocabulary. And the turpentine. I can still smell its pungent odor filling the living room as she was mixing a minimal color palette to start painting.

"Come on, have a try, this blank canvas is for you."

I could barely hold the paintbrush, and after a few brushstrokes, I stopped. I was starting to feel overwhelmed by her expectations, mine as well, and I did not want to show her my unease.

I fed my soul by watching her work on her piece of art. I swallowed her tranquility and sipped the shades of earthy tones slowly filling the image, but the deep feelings of frustration and inability had forcibly taken me back into the past.

In my mouth, I savored the bitter flavor of yet another 'first time' in my life.

In the following days, I kept on thinking about the possibility of making art. I was able to find some old stuff I had used in my teenage years, but colored pencils and oil pastels did not attract my interest at all. Painting, on the contrary, was exciting.

Mixing colors was like creating rainbows and giving a physical dimension to magic.

My then-dominant engineer personality lit a lamp by suggesting that I could find precise instructions to mix colors, and that voice whispering, "You are stubborn enough to learn how to paint" was so loud that I asked

You are stubborn enough

Cristina if she could buy some art supplies for me. Like a belated Christmas day, I got my tubes of oil paint, long red paintbrushes, linseed oil, turpentine and a wooden palette.

"And they lived happily ever after."

It did not go that way.

Indeed, I have to say that I was not able to use the art practice to find relief from the external pressure. Not knowing anything about color theory and technique, painting soon became a pressure itself because I could not find proper time to study, experiment, make mistakes and learn.

My bohemian dream of the artist's life was crushed on the rocks of my family's needs, my full-time job, my exhausting routine, my loneliness. It was a small, light boat unable to resist the windy storms.

First time, last time.

I stored those supplies in a corner of my big house and forgot about them.

It took me three more years, and many tears, to get to the point where I heard that voice whispering to me again, pushing me to art practice.

But differently from the past, this time I experienced a deeper awareness of the purpose that the voice was bringing. I did not assume I felt called to make art with the purpose of painting masterpieces at any cost.

My desire to learn how to paint now had no foundation but a burning desire for self-affirmation.

Making a short summary of my life until that moment, and seeing my life as a movie, I could clearly see that I had lived immersed in literature since I learnt how to read. My daily food consisted of books and museums.

I was aware I had shifted to technical knowledge and science to find a well-paid job without being ashamed of it. I had devoted all my energy to my family and career.

But I had lost me. I was a pale imitation of myself.

I desperately needed beauty to fill my days, to be my solace!

Art would have been my way. To speak to myself and to the world.

My husband has this mantra, "No one can change your life if you do not help yourself and start changing it." At first, when he told me that, as I was complaining about my lack of enthusiasm and motivation towards everything, I thought he was rude.

In my vision, not everyone is strong enough to fight against the constituted order of social conventions and family boundaries, and break the invisible chains that block us and keep us far from imagination and action.

I decided to take responsibility for my happiness and growth as a human being.

I had another first time with painting, which was not the last.

And now, if I think about myself, I just see a curly girl holding a book in one hand, as a reminder of my first love for words, a paintbrush in the other as a symbol of my last love for art.

First love, last love.

I do not remember what loneliness means.

I am completely surrounded by the warm embrace of my enormous love for portraiture, and when I paint, I find myself in a timeless dimension where all is forgiveness and possibility. I create a deep emotional connection to the soul of the person that I paint, so that the portrait is not mere physical appearance, but becomes an image of the soul.

Day by day I discover my voice as an artist and I change the world one painting at a time.

I am a living mixture of empathy and excitement. I carry with me the shadows of my past and dilute them with the colors on my palette to bring women my message of authenticity and love.

I don't hide myself anymore.

Do not call me "Madam".

Do not label me as an engineer, mother, wife.

Do not call me artist.

Just call me by my name.

Elisa, the soul painter.

When I draw the first line of a face, I feel all the love in the world conveyed in my hand.

Elisa Colangeli

Grow and Reflect with Elisa

I experienced that making art cares for my emotional self, and by doing so I am more compassionate to those around me. Since I believe that we were all born creatives, I would love to guide you in some activities to help you to rediscover your artistic source and access creative capacity for personal growth, healing and joy. This will help you dispel common myths about artistic creativity, remove barriers and obstacles to your creative wisdom, and learn to believe that you are an artist.

Exactly as I did.

Step 1

Cut out some illustrations of parts of the body (legs, arms, eyes, hair ...), backgrounds, clothes, symbols, flowers, animals and writings from old magazines that catch your attention, and collect them. You can print single images from the internet if you feel called by a specific one.

Give yourself time to have a considerable number of images, because you will love the opportunity to choose. When you have many clippings, you can organize your items by dividing them by color or theme.

Afterwards, find a picture of yourself, it could be a photo of the whole figure or simply your face. Cut out your shape.

On the white space that follows, start playing with the images that you have collected coupling them to your face, or body, or both. Rotate, turn them around, select what you want to keep, and cut them again to adapt them the scene you are developing.

Create a new image of yourself. Don't make it plausible at any cost. Change yourself into a mermaid, a fairy, a goddess, or embrace adventure by flying on a hot air balloon.

There are no limits to the magic you can create by juxtaposing images.

This is a chance to distance yourself from reality, and you deserve to savor freedom.

Once you set the composition in the most effective way, you can glue the cut-outs to the paper.

Close your eyes for a couple of minutes, touching the paper that you collaged, feeling the smoothness, the edges and the smell of ink and glue.

Open your eyes and come back to the present moment. You are ready to call the image by its name. Write it down, filling the blank space in the following line, and then say out loud:

I, ..., am the deliberate creator of this piece of art that I name:

" .... "

Step 2

Now that you have experienced how your perception can detach from the physical level to enter a more intimate and spiritual side, I invite you to reflect about your inner world. You have an emotional landscape with its own shadows and lights, your soul being soaked in a variety of colors, or perhaps in a monochromatic tint.

What does your soul palette look like? Which colors would you choose to represent your soul?

Sit quietly for some time and evaluate your current state of mind, considering what feelings and emotions are with you at the moment. Think of a landscape that could represent your feelings, like a metaphor allowing you to explore your emotions symbolically.

On paper, sketch with a pencil the lines of what you visualized in the background, middle ground and foreground. Take a small set of watercolors and a paintbrush, and add blocks of color to your landscape. Up to you to choose between strong and diluted colors.

Add a short description for your landscape.

I feel like I am in a special place, where:

_____

_____

_____

_____

_____

_____

_____

Step 3

Have you got a particular flower, animal, or fruit that you feel connected to, and you don't know why?

Maybe you see that image in recurring dreams, or you feel it has some hidden meanings to explore.

It could be your archetypal symbol, which means that throughout history that particular item has been given a specific meaning in different cultures, and it now has a universal intrinsic value. It is now an archetype.

Let's embrace curiosity and investigate a symbol you love, answering some questions:

* Where and when do you meet this symbol?
* What is its meaning in ancient cultures all over the world?

* ★ Can it be found in paintings, sculptures?
* ★ What is its purpose and daily use today?
* ★ What does it tell you? How can you incorporate your archetypal symbol into your life?

I recommend you use Pinterest to create a board where you can collect all kinds of images related to the symbol. Summarize your journey of discovery in the space below.

My symbol is:

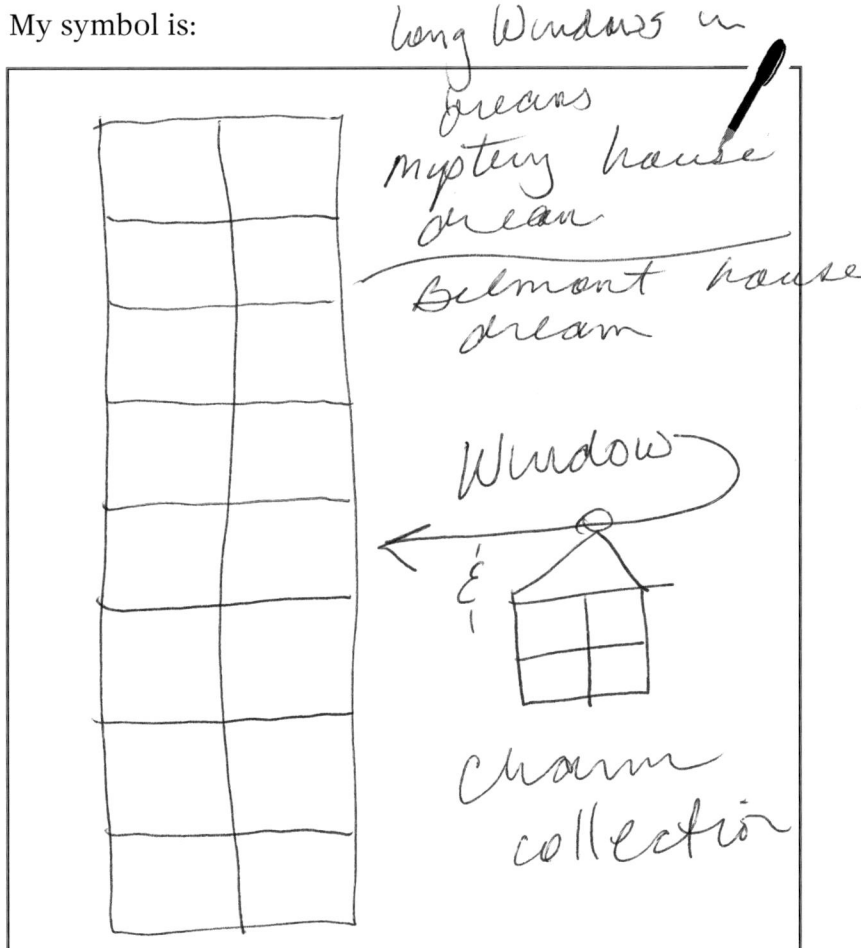

How would it be to have a "soul logo" incorporating the image of your archetypal symbol to strengthen your wonderful interior qualities?

Sketch the symbol with a pencil in the circle opposite, choosing a reference picture that you like. You don't have to copy the item in all the details, since the logo is a simplified version of the reference.

Add your name and an adjective or phrase that describes you. Not labels like wife or daughter, which have social implications, but "the warrior" or "the merciful" which is all about your essence.

Have fun and celebrate your inner beauty.

You can keep your creativity going by joining my art hub on Facebook. It is a community where every member is called to develop the creative side of the soul. I will be happy to welcome you and see you grow along your artist's way.

Request to access here:
www.facebook.com/groups/367460968546298

This is my GIFT to you: https://youtu.be/QsqPE768bWE

CONTACT ELISA

 www.facebook.com/elisa.colangeli.56

 www.instagram.com/elisacolangeliart

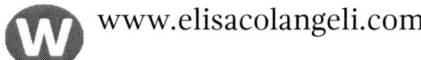 www.elisacolangeli.com

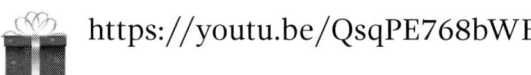 https://youtu.be/QsqPE768bWE

Space for your thoughts ...

....

....

....

....

....

....

....

....

....

....

....

....

....

....

....

....

....

....

I am a woman who is here to change the script on what a sexy and successful woman looks, sounds and feels like.

TINA ELOISE

Tina Eloise is an international feminine embodiment and liberation mentor.

She is the creator of The Sacred Scream Ceremony & Somatic Shadow Work which is a powerful modality using the body and expression to heal and create the life you want.

Over the past 10 years, Tina has gone from being a Reiki Healer riddled with horrific childhood trauma, rage, and shame to becoming a renowned core wound specialist and helping 1000's of women across the globe to become empowered and liberated throughout their lives so they experience pleasure in all forms.

She uses a unique blend of psychological, emotional, somatic, spiritual and energetic modalities that she has learned and used on herself to create massive changes not only in her life but also in the lives of her clients and students.

Tina is a keen tantric and master energy healer; she is a firm believer that the key to healing and expansion is through the body and self-expression.

As an overweight, post-menopausal, neuro-diverse, potty-mouthed cockney witch who was always told she was too much or felt she was not enough, Tina is here to help women rewrite the script of what it means to be a sexy and successful woman.

Tina believes EVERY woman, no matter her past, body type or age deserves to be seen, heard and adored for the goddess she is.

Tina's Secrets

Ok, so I have stood on an ostrich egg in South Africa –
yup both feet and taken a ride on one – on an ostrich
that is, not on an egg!

I have had sex in a graveyard (by accident).

Me and my friends in primary school recorded a song
that got to number 49 in the charts (I think it was
number 49).

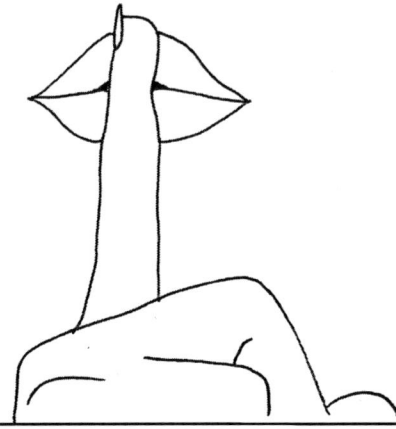

Dark Familiarity

Hey gorgeous reader, so you have come across my story and are expecting me to take you on a journey of empowerment by sharing my lived experiences.

Truth is, I do not know where to start or what to write.

So many tragic things have happened in my life that I have had to overcome. Child abuse, teenage homelessness, countless sexual assaults, teenage pregnancy, domestic violence, drug and alcohol addiction, suicide, bulimia, mental health breakdowns and cancer.

Geeez ... that was an intense 35 years wouldn't you say!?!

So which one do I choose from that bucket of worms to relay my story of survival, healing and empowerment?

It's hard to pick, and I only have 1500 words to engage and inspire you. And to be honest with you, they all are linked to each other.

No incident or experience is ever an isolated incident. It's always history repeating itself in one form or another.

Until we are aware of our wounding.

Until we face our darkness.

Until we express the unspoken, we will keep living the same stories of our childhood, and our parents' childhood and so on and so forth.

I would love to tell you that healing is easy, it just takes belief, change, a bit of positive thinking and it's all gone. But that would be a lie. Healing is frigging hard.

So where do I start ...

What story shall I share?

I suppose it would have to be my biggest and hardest healing journey to date, the one that took me to the depths of hell and made me nearly lose my mind.

Yup, that's the one.

So dear reader, I am going to tell you about my journey with my body and how tantra saved my life.

You see, at the beginning of my healing journey, when the cancer hit at 35, I found freedom to dive into all the things I wanted to but which my career and toxic drama-filled life had never allowed me to. I like to think of that time as a holiday from being me.

I fell straight into the big hitters, *The Secret*, Gabby Bernstein, Abraham Hicks – you know the like. And they were awesome.

I was a manifesting powerhouse when I got better. Learnt all the modalities – reiki, NLP, EFT, coaching. You name it, I was in there like a kid on a TikTok trend. It was amazing.

And then ...

It all went to crap. I got ill, my income dried up and I had debt collectors hunting me down. And nothing I had learnt was working. I was doing all the things, affirmations, meditations, tapping my face off. And nothing was working.

And suddenly ...

All the stuff I had been running away from in my childhood came rushing back up to the surface. I was left feeling that I was so messed up I couldn't manifest a cuppa tea let alone my dream life.

I was thinking that there was a part of me that hated myself so much that it created the reality I was in. The suicidal thoughts came back and I got so scared. So went to the doc's, got some talking therapy and started to rebuild my life.

This is when the healing really started.

This is when I faced my body and sexual energy.

This is when I started my journey into my feminine.

I have come to realise that when I first started my healing journey way back then, ten years ago now, I was still running away. I was still numbing. I had replaced drugs and alcohol with affirmations, mantras and positive thinking.

Anything to keep me away from my body and the pain that she held there. I kept seeing signs and nudges to connect with her through dancing or somatic work but I would sabotage myself or tell myself no, maybe later. Another time. When really I felt intimidated, not good enough, not feminine enough, too fat, too common to join any of the tantra classes, or dance classes or burlesque.

So when I realised post breakdown that I needed to do this journey ... hello ... what the hell was it going to take for me to do this.

I found an online, female teacher, knowing that I would feel safer with a woman, and started the journey from there.

I was surprised, tantra wasn't all about sex. It was about connecting with your body. Of course, there is sex in there and connecting your sexual energy. But ultimately it is connection with your body.

It has been the most gruelling thing I have ever been through, but the most rewarding. Hidden away in my body I met, embraced and loved that little girl wanting to be loved, that teenager who didn't know how to nurture herself, that woman who sold her worth for warped toxic affection and misguided love.

That woman who believed she was so disgusting and held onto so much shame she would never love her body and couldn't look at herself in the mirror. That female so scared of intimacy that she abused her body to escape self-inquiry.

The daughter so resentful towards her mother that she disassociated from her body (anything to get away from the feminine). This stuff was so hard to face.

I have cried and felt sick so many times, as I could feel the shame, hatred, disgust and rage, the putrid energetic web of emotion and beliefs in my body rise up and pour out.

I felt rage for my childhood lost.

I felt sorrow for my younger selves.

I mourned the little girl with dreams of being saved that never came true.

I felt guilt for the woman she became and things she had done.

And I voiced it all.

I gave myself full permission to say all the words that I was holding onto.

I screamed.

Punched.

Kicked.

Shouted.

Into pillows, cushions, beds and sofas.

I allowed myself to feel the full spectrum of emotions at full force, until my face was red raw and swollen with tears and my stomach felt cavernous from the outpouring of emotion.

I forgave.

Forgave myself for not believing that I was worth more.

Forgave myself for not loving myself for so many years.

Forgave myself for not seeing the beauty I hold within my being.

Forgave myself for not respecting, caressing and loving my bountiful body.

And then, I felt peace, love, connection and safety. All the things I craved for so long.

I have no doubt more tears will come as I naturally dismantle the not worthy gene of shame and guilt as I journey more into my relationship with my body and sexuality.

I am ready and open to explore all that may come to the surface. Until the dark familiarity of my shadow rises and, as a post-menopausal 46-year-old, obese, potty-mouthed witch, I will be loving and exciting my body at any chance I get. And I will be the walking, talking proof that the divine feminine comes in many forms and it doesn't matter what you look like, your age or your background.

You are

Sassy

Sensual

Magickal

& Magnetic.

And you get to be sexy and successful just as you are!

Big Juicy Luv

Tina

To truly tap into your feminine essence you have to feel. Feel it all. Feel it all, the full spectrum for emotions.

You can't truly experience the high if you don't allow yourself to feel, express and move through the low.

Tina Eloise

Grow and Reflect with Tina

So, are you ready to start your journey of reconnecting with your body gorgeous?

Don't worry, I am not going to ask you to whip out your sex toys – unless you want to of course (wink, wink).

No, we are going to show her some love. Get to know her a bit better.

We are going to be retraining your mind to see the beauty that is hidden in plain sight.

More often than not we look in the mirror and see only our flaws. So by doing this exercise on a regular basis we will reverse that and before you know it, you will be walking past every mirror giving yourself a wink and thinking to yourself what a gorgeous being you are. You may also give yourself a cheeky pat on the bum like I do. Ha ha ... that's optional of course.

So grab your favourite pen, put on some music, light a candle or incense (the feminine loves ritual).

And grab a mirror, or sit in front of one.

1. First, take a deep breath, put your hand on your heart centre and bring your awareness to that space.

    See how it feels to be touching that space, how does it feel on your hand? How does your chest feel at the touch of your hand?

Keep taking a few breaths until you get the nudge to stop.

See, that wasn't hard. That was the warm up.

Now it is very important that you follow your intuition here. Whatever part of your body comes up first is the right one to work with.

2. Now I want you to think about a part of your body that you love (you may need a mirror for this work) and describe it to me, what do you love about it, what makes that part of your body so special?

3. Now I want you to think about a part of your body that you do not like. Describe it, let it all out – what is it that you do not like about that part of the body. What is it you tell yourself?

4. Now I want you to write down all things that part of your body (the part you don't like) does for you? Why is that part of your body so needed?

How are you feeling now? Well done. It's hard to face those parts of ourselves. Do you feel shocked by some of the beliefs that may have come up?

One last thing, I am not the kind of witch who leaves a sister hanging. I want you to reconnect with your heart centre again like you did before. However, this time I want you to bring to mind that part of the body that you dislike. You can look in a mirror to do this, or do it with your eyes closed.

I want you to connect with it and see how she feels. What is she saying to you?

Maybe you need to apologise.

Maybe you need to forgive yourself.

And whilst your hand is on your heart, I want you to send soooooo much love to that part of your body. Repeating in your mind:

I LOVE YOU, I AM HERE, I AM LISTENING.

With every inhale, just breathe into that space and with every exhale release all the negativity and outdated beliefs stored there. You may get some resistance to this part but I urge you to lean into that edge. Keep going.

When you get the intuitive nudge to stop, stop.

And that's it.

I am celebrating you connecting with your body in such a loving and intimate way. I encourage you to do this process at least a few times a week and take note of what you start to see when you look in the mirror

This is my GIFT to you:
https://www.tinaeloise.com/freebie-vault-su

CONTACT TINA

 www.facebook.com/tina.eloise.76

 www.instagram.com/tina_eloise_london/

 www.tinaeloise.com

 www.tinaeloise.com/freebie-vault-su

Space for your thoughts ...

I am a woman who found happiness uncovering her inner brilliance and embracing all that she is, and who wants to lead you to do the same.

GAIA SCIARANGHELLA

Gaia is an intuitive, a mentor for life transformation, a guide and educator, who specializes in practices for mind-body balance, energy healing, spiritual awareness and personal development. She is the founder of The Awakening of Gaia and is based in Boston, USA.

She has training and experience in both traditional and complementary medicine. Through her unique way of blending science-backed holistic medicine modalities with novel spiritual techniques, she is on a mission to empower spiritually conscious and soul-led women to access the language of their souls in daily life, establishing a life-long rapport with their inner power and intuition. She wants to guide them to be leaders in all aspects of their lives, boosting their self-confidence to live a more joyful, uncomplicated and deeply satisfying life.

Gaia is the creator of a methodology to awake our Inner Brilliance, our inner energy propelling us to act in the world with vibrancy and confidence.

She has proudly inspired countless people to blossom in

life and be more in touch with their inner wisdom, both through her online presence and in-person work.

When not working, Gaia enjoys long walks in nature, exploring new restaurants, dancing, and making new friends, and she would love to connect with you as well.

Gaia's Secrets

I moved to the US by myself with my life packed in just two pieces of luggage.

I took the Sugarloaf Mountain (the famous Pão de Açúcar) cable car in Rio de Janeiro, Brazil, at sunset, reaching an altitude of more than 390 m to enjoy a 360-degree view of the city.

I danced Argentine tango in Buenos Aires, and ate authentic Spanish paella and *churros con chocolate* in the Plaza Mayor in Madrid.

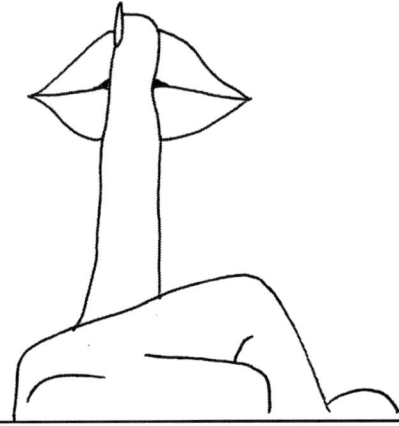

The Right Side of the Window

That day I had the confirmation something odd was going on with me. Once again, the professor missed the class. And once again, I knew beforehand that it was going to happen. I had a vague, undistinguished feeling someone was coming to sub for his class, but I had no idea where that feeling was coming from.

I knew when someone was lying to me, what decisions they were going to take and why. It was as if I was able to read people's behavior. I was concealing this uncomfortable feeling of being different under the justification that it was just common sense, although it was not all that common. It was a sense other people were missing. What could I do with those insights? And why were they coming to me? What was I supposed to do with them?

This sense of knowing had been accompanying me since I was very little. My parents still cherish a little piece of paper I scribbled on when I was seven. I was playing with my dolls, pretending to prescribe them medicines, when I stuck the title of "Doctor" in front of my name. My curiosity to understand how things work and my love for science finally met with my life purpose: helping people, finding solutions to make them feel better, to improve their health.

It was a natural consequence to bury my unhelpful sense of knowing to follow the conventional path, the only one I knew at that time. In this way, I became a scientist.

My determination brought me to the USA to be a researcher at a prestigious institution in Boston. But that was not enough for me, and it was not a matter of ambition. There are people who want to be in prestigious positions and are never satisfied with what they have as they need to be recognized by others to feel they are important. But that wasn't me. Not even climbing the professional ladder was bringing me joy. I had accrued many recognitions as a perfect student since I was in elementary school, as the walls of the house I left in my home country can still attest. Why was I never feeling fulfilled with what I had?

Over the years I was able to get the professional positions I wanted, to improve my financial situation. I was loved by my family and friends. I was young. I had good health. In short, I had everything a person could have to call herself happy. And yet, I was filled with a sense of emptiness inside. I was constantly asking myself "Is that it? Or there is more to life?"

Something dissonant was starting to get louder and louder. Like when different instruments of an orchestra play each one according to their own lyric, and the resulting music is out of tune.

Like today, the sky was gray and it was pouring rain. I was standing in front of the window; the air was cold, as if to reflect the chilling cold I was feeling. "So what's missing?" I asked myself while gasping for air, a sense of anxiety and fear growing. I was waiting for what I did not know. I was hoping for the future to bring me a change, waiting for something to appear, maybe a helping hand. The anxiety became despair: I wanted to be a different person. That woman I knew was lost in the abyss of my soul; the woman

I knew existed, but had never met. And how did it feel to be happy and contempt? Now I know the despair was exacerbated by waiting for something to change outside myself. For this reason, I had the illusion I was not in control, nor had any power to change my circumstances.

The day my beloved grandma passed away was the saddest day of my life. We had a true bond. We were two peas in a pod. She was able to get me more than anyone else, and she shared with me the ability to sense people's intentions, to get out-of-nowhere "intuitive hits", as I lately came to understand. I was sure we had a connection that was going beyond time and space. And I had validation of our special interconnectedness when I started to physically feel her loving presence with me. At first, I thought I was losing my mind; my imagination was playing tricks. Then I started to feel what she would have said about a given situation, but I knew hopelessness and desperation were not playing any part in this. And I knew our earthly way of communicating with each other was taking on a whole new meaning.

From that point on, this became our new way to connect, which for me opened a new window through which I could see the world. My grandma was lending me a helping hand through that window. Everything became clear to me. The totality of my talents could not be ignored if I wanted to be happy. Who was I really, and how I could use my talents to help people? These new revelations brought me shame. I felt like a failure. After all the years of study, many of those desires no longer belonged to me. I felt like a fraud, and tears could not wash away the disappointment I felt towards myself. I had not been happy until that point because I had taken the easiest and most socially acceptable professional path, and I was defining myself through the labels I fabricated. Admitting I was a different person felt like a defeat to me. Now I understand there was no blame I could put on myself, while lovingly mumbling "Schools do not teach you how to really be yourself in the world".

Happiness was a thread I had to untangle first and foremost within myself. The same determination which brought me to the US was now serving to unravel my inner thread, with which I could tighten all the parts of me I was no longer willing to deny. I had finally found the strength to shake away years of unhappiness. It was true. I had deceived myself for years. Not pretending to be someone else, but denying parts of me I did not want to acknowledge. Refusing them. I didn't know I could be so much more than I expected to be.

I was ready to grab with both hands parts of my personality that I had forgotten for years. Not only deciding to be maybe funnier, more spontaneous, more open and trusting towards people, ready to change my personal style or look, but embracing all aspects of being human, and recognizing the most fundamental piece of this puzzle, my spiritual side. It became the foundations of the house I was desperately trying to build.

In fact, my grandma's gift was a more precious one: it made me realize that accepting my spiritual essence was essential to my happiness. Not just the spiritual essence outside of myself, the something or someone we turn to for guidance and help, making us forget we have personal responsibility for our life choices. Rather, the spiritual nature residing in me. Inside each one of us. Available, tangible more than we are taught growing up.

My world was not made only of a jumble of matter. I was not only flesh and bones. I not only had a logical brain. My life filtered through logic was a life without passion, joy and excitement. I was made of emotions. The modern culture I was living in was not accepting of those emotions, and I was constantly trying to suffocate them to be accepted in my profession. My world was made as well of the energy pulsating through all human beings, an energy that cannot be destroyed when our body ceases to exist.

To my amazement, my spiritual side was not as abstract as I thought. It was not about sitting in solitude on a mountain, or retiring to an ascetic life, eating raw buds and waiting for an illumination to strike me. It couldn't be further from this image. On the contrary, it was helping me to stay more present and attuned to my day-to-day life, to receive with a generous smile every opportunity falling on the path of my mortal existence. And in welcoming my spiritual nature, I was learning to trust my intuition, that force that was leading me to uncover my worth, to let my inner brilliance shine out.

As I was starting to align my inner desires, talents, strengths and power my life took a whole new direction, towards the way I was going to live in my external world. I found the strength to achieve what I'd thought was impossible, and from that came freedom. And with the freedom, the burning desire to bring the same liberation to others. To help them as I had desired since I was a child.

A veil lifted from my eyes, and I was able to see a world that had always been in front of me, but I could not really notice. And with that veil, my despair and dissatisfaction were lifted as well. They left me like they had never been there, making plenty of room for joy and expectation for the future. Earlier, I was waiting at the window to spot what the future could bring me. But the future could not bring me something I was not willing to bring to myself. Now, I was in control of who I decided to be.

The key to unlocking a world of happiness was inside of me. The key was to fully accept myself. Only after that, was I able to really love myself. Listening to my soul's calling was the way to make peace with that little girl, whose gifts were too much for her world. It was the way to fulfill my purpose of leading others to find their own key. Each one of us has a key inside to open a world of joy.

My everyday best practice consists of remembering that my spiritual side gives me strength. And no matter what happens outside of myself, my strength will always support me. As a result, compromising, settling for less, weakening my boundaries, devaluing my self-worth come much harder for me now.

My journey to myself continues to this day, and I am still gazing out of that window. But I no longer wait for the future to bring me surprises. I wait enthusiastically for what I am able to create every day, for how I will evolve, grow and transform each day.

And now every day is a juicy and flavorful fruit waiting only to be enjoyed.

Happiness comes from fully loving yourself.

Loving yourself comes from fully accepting yourself – all parts of yourself, including those you do not want to see, or do not know you have.

Gaia Sciaranghella

Grow and Reflect with Gaia

I hope my story inspires you to look for all the aspects of yourself and embrace the wholeness of who you are.

I would love for you to follow me now on a short journey to intuitively sense and reconnect with those parts, including your spiritual nature. With practice, it will become easier and easier to start perceiving and integrating all aspects of who you are, to make the most out of your life.

1. Choose a place where you can sit quietly without distractions. Light a candle as a reminder you have a light inside, which I call your "inner brilliance", that is meant to be shared with the world through all you do. At any point in the exploration, you can pause and jot down some notes to keep track of your thoughts and feelings.

2. With your eyes closed:

   * Start feeling your BODY first. Do you feel any sensation?

   * Which EMOTIONS are coming up for you today? Do you feel any particular emotion localized in any part of your body? Observe...

   * Then be aware of any thoughts passing through your MIND.

   * After that, try to sense your surrounding space and objects or living beings (plants, animals, people).

Do you feel their presence? You are feeling their energetic presence through your own ENERGY field.

★ Now imagine the light of the candle being situated in the core of your body, pulsing according to every in-breath and out-breath you take. This represents your SPIRITUAL essence, and the source of your inner wisdom. What does it want to tell you today?

3. Now reflect: which part of the exploration did you find more difficult to do? Which part offered you more resistance? This is the part of you needing more care and attention to better develop.

Repeat this exercise out in nature and notice how (or if) it is different. Repeat it several days in a row and write down in the space opposite all your impressions and the way you are now seeing and responding to life challenges, and the level of calm and joy you are experiencing.

This is my GIFT to you:
www.awakeningofgaia.com/freegift/

CONTACT GAIA

www.facebook.com/gaia.sciaran

www.facebook.com/groups/551205023016890

www.awakeningofgaia.com

www.awakeningofgaia.com/freegift/

Space for your thoughts ...

....

....

....

....

....

....

....

....

....

....

....

....

....

....

....

....

....

I am a woman who allowed herself to see and own her beauty when I moved across the Atlantic Ocean and learned how to see my reflection through the eyes of a Makeup Artist.

SARA ANNES MATOS

Sara is a guide, a speaker and an artist based in London. She aims to help people expand into freedom of self-expression by embracing all that they are and unleashing their hidden potency.

Her masterclass *Fall in love with your face*™ is a safe space for people to fall in love with their reflection in the mirror and heal those parts that were deemed unacceptable. Her online membership *Seasons of the Rose Academy*™ is a community focused on guiding people to be who they truly are, through the seasons, and to explore their creative expression.

Sara loves dancing, taking walks in nature and having deep conversations with her friends. She enjoys connecting and collaborating with people. Reach out to her at info@ saraannesmatos.com.

Sara's Secrets

In 2022, I started being referred to as "the Sauce", after creating a reel dancing to the song *Sauce* by Naïka, inviting people to own their own potency.

I won a local Kizomba competition at a dance party in Toronto, dancing with a woman, after no men accepted our invitation to participate.

I once pranked my grandmother by convincing her I had pooed on the floor of a carnival shop, without even taking my shorts off. We laughed about it together for years.

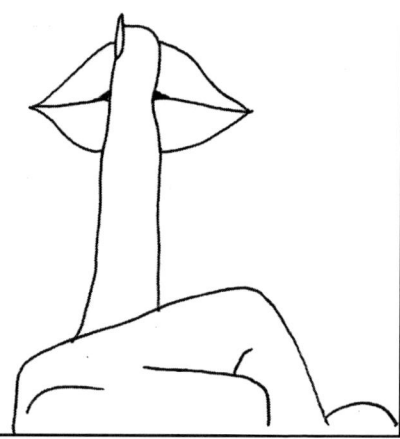

The Girl Standing in the Mirror

Something incredibly powerful awakened inside me the day I finally decided to take that salsa course for beginners at my local dance school. The sound of the clave moved through me, calling my body to sway in a way that I didn't know I craved. Like a primal beat, connecting me to Earth saying "You are here to stay, you are here to take up space". It was raw, feminine and potent.

Since I was a child, I believed that bad things would happen if I got noticed and took up that space. I remember at seven years old entering the bathroom at my parents' house. The silence was eating me alive. I had convinced myself no one would ever understand what I was going through. The thing about suppressed shame is that it festers in the shadows. I felt so alone. As far as I was concerned, I was the only one with these feelings, this knot in my throat, this inner voice telling me on a loop how ugly and disgusting I was. I gazed at the mirror and allowed my tears to fall. I didn't like her very much, the girl staring back at me. She was disgusting, a shell of the carefree child I once knew.

Everything about me was wrong. It surely didn't help to go to a very small private school where I would stay until I was 16. When you spend your childhood and most of your teenage years in a bubble, with little to no diversity, it is easy to assume you are the worst person in the whole world. My uniqueness was a flaw. A potency that should be hidden. I believed no one would notice if I was gone, so I chose to make myself invisible.

I learned very early on that the best way to function in my reality was to be a people pleaser, put my needs behind others, stay silent, be obedient and submissive, whilst a tornado built within. I didn't dare to confront authority figures or step outside the lines.

Vulnerability was a weakness and I didn't know how to self-soothe, so I chose to avoid conversations I knew would make me cry. The ones that perhaps mattered the most, including stating my needs and setting boundaries. I also didn't know I had a choice in how others treated me. I believed I deserved abuse.

"I have a problem" were the four words I shared more than once with my mother, on the way home from school. My primary teacher told me I had no personality – like dough with no salt. My close friend mocked my feet. Someone that I deeply cared about made comments about my appearance. My family told me I was selfish. *One time* was all it took for me to buy into their opinions of me. The seeds of not-enoughness had been planted. I was constantly seeking permission to be me. A pretty dangerous reality to live in.

There were good things about that school, but also a lot of emotional abuse happening in the background. One of the experiences that stood out to me the most was when I was placed in the middle of a circle, composed of my classmates, and the teacher encouraged them to judge me. That memory popped up time and time again when I was setting myself free from the fear of humiliation and shame under the spotlight.

Being told I was loved or pretty bounced off, just like rain hitting a waterproof jacket.

I remember in my early teens my father teaching me the basics of cha-cha and mambo, my feet on top of his. I had been taking dance classes since I was 12, but it was only when salsa found me at the age of 21 that the beast was released. It was like coming home to a daring feminine nature I didn't know existed. My sensuality was ignited.

On the first day of the fourth year of my Integrated Master's in Biomedical Engineering, it all hit me. Salsa had turned on a light switch on all the ways I had denied myself the option to live a life that was worth living, my career being one of them.

Life Worth Living

In tears, I confided in a good friend of mine who suggested I take a break to figure things out. My mother, who always supported my desire to be an artist, stayed silent as my father told me how he wouldn't support my decision. He would stop supporting my sister who was now in New York studying to become a professional dancer. I cared about keeping a relationship with him and that whatever I chose didn't impact my sister. So I stayed. That was the night my inner rebel started driving the wheel. I realised that no matter how much I tried, I could never win.

The months that followed cracked me open and shattered years of putting him on a pedestal. After all, he was a human just like me, with a healing journey in front of him. Rage and anger kept me going. I would give my all to the remaining years of my master's and then I would do whatever I wanted. I just had no clue what. The questions "Who am I? What am I good at? What do I like?" played in my head.

It was not too long after that, that my mother heard about a small makeup workshop that would take place inside a clothing shop on a Saturday afternoon. I don't think I even owned a mascara or eyeliner at that point. My reality exploded. I was the painter and the face was the canvas!

I started watching makeup tutorials every day. The voice of Lisa Eldridge sometimes played in the background as I studied for my exams. She believed in enhancing natural beauty and her artistry was like no other. Inspired by her, my research started and that's how I found the College of Makeup Art and Design in Toronto, Canada. Bit by bit I allowed myself to dream that the impossible was possible ... *What if I could be this happy every day?*

When a year or so later my father asked me what I wanted to do after I finished my master's, I replied "I am going to become a makeup artist." He laughed, because he believed no one was going to respect me, but I had already made up my mind. Nothing in my energy asked for permission. It was just me, my desires and my truth.

A month after I presented my dissertation, in 2015, I was on a flight to Toronto. As I sat in my allotted seat, I realised the impact of this choice. It was not just about the pursuit of happiness and fulfilling my dreams. It was about new beginnings. With no one telling me how to be, I had the chance to explore myself fully.

The first time I saw the college with my own eyes, I cried with joy. Studying felt like reading a magazine. Every weekend, I gladly sat at the coffee shop with a cappuccino and a steaming blueberry muffin, whilst reading about all the wonderful topics makeup artistry had to offer. I was in heaven.

What if I could be this happy every day?

The more I learned about the face and the more I looked at my reflection, the less critical I became. Every time we would practice on each other, I had a fellow student inches from my face. Exposed, with nowhere to hide, I allowed myself to drop the barriers and trust that I would be ok. When my classmates started complimenting me, I realised I was so used to scanning my reflection for what was wrong that I completely missed the mark. Before I knew it, that waterproof jacket became more permeable as acknowledged my unique beauty and started loving my face.

The different parts of us that are yearning for our love communicate with us in many ways. It was not that long ago that I looked at a picture of myself in my early teens and wanted to turn it around with disgust. This reinforced my idea that loving our reflection in the mirror is so much more than appreciating our external beauty. It's about courageously choosing to bring back the aspects of ourselves that stayed neglected in the shadows and creating safety for them to exist right now exactly as they are. This is what freedom means to me.

I carry in my heart that seven-year-old and all the other parts of me I have retrieved so far. When I enter the bathroom and gaze at the mirror, I love her, I love the woman staring back at me. Unruly eyebrows, sleepy look and all ... she is the sauce. Courageously, she rose like a phoenix from the ashes time and time again; she refused to sit in her pain, she knew she deserved to come home to herself.

I now know that lack of awareness often leads people to project their own suppressed shame onto others, without understanding what drove their actions in the first place. We have all played that role. I had to forgive myself for the times I did it and those times when I allowed it. Those harsh words that I heard? They were never about me.

When you take off the cloak of shame protecting your vulnerability you access your truth and potency. It's not just about you anymore, you become the powerful healing tool you came here to be. Leading by example and creating ripple effects of healing. One thing I am sure, no one can be or do, who you came here to be, or do. So it's time to come out of the shadows and expand into infinite possibilities.

out of the Shadows

Loving your reflection in the mirror is so much more than appreciating your external beauty. It's about courageously choosing to bring back the aspects of yourself that were deemed unacceptable and creating safety for them to exist in your reality exactly as they are.

Sara Annes Matos

Grow and Reflect with Sara

Gorgeous being, when I wrote this story my intention was to bring you expansion beyond this reality. I invite you to close your eyes now and imagine a door with the word "freedom" written on it. This is your moment to stop waiting for permission and enter the realm of infinite possibilities.

To open the door, you must set your own intention and state "I choose this". Beautiful. You are about to go on a journey to fall in love with your reflection in the mirror and retrieve some of your dormant gifts!

You will need a mirror, a journal and a pen. Make sure you are somewhere that feels safe, where you can drop your guard and deeply connect with yourself. All the parts of you are welcome here. They will communicate with you in different ways such as emotions, feelings, thoughts and bodily sensations. You don't need to force anything to happen. Remember that you are in charge of your own pace and how deep you go. You are encouraged to return to these exercises as inspired.

Ready? Let's begin.

I choose this

1. Set a timer for five minutes, play a soothing song (suggestion: *I release* by Beautiful Chorus). Position the mirror so that you can see your face and gaze at your reflection. If any thought of criticism or emotions arise, simply acknowledge them. These are different parts of you communicating. Your task is to allow them and become the observer. Journal about this experience.

2. It's time to meet the part(s) of you who crave your love the most, and heal by becoming the parent they always craved and never had. I invite you to listen to the meditation I have created for you at www.saraannesmatos.com/falling-in-love-with-you. Then come back and write about your experience and the birthright gifts you've retrieved.

3. Bring back the mirror. Start by noticing if anything changed compared to the first step. Then I would like you to scan your reflection for what is right about you. What is your favourite thing about your face? Own it by sharing it with a friend.

Become the parent you never had you craved.

CONTACT SARA

 www.facebook.com/saraannesmatos

 www.instagram.com/saraannesmatos/

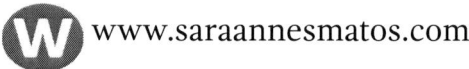 www.saraannesmatos.com

 www.saraannesmatos.com/falling-in-love-with-you

Space for your thoughts ...

....

....

....

....

....

....

....

....

....

....

....

....

....

....

....

....

....

....

I am a woman who dares to question what we're told.

DOROTHY WATT

Dorothy Watt is a transformational homeopath and holistic wellness advocate.

Dorothy grew up intending to be a research scientist. However, during her Cambridge University science degree she decided she preferred working with people, celebrating their uniqueness and individual differences.

Education, with its focus on human interaction, seemed a more attractive choice and a successful career in education as a teacher, published researcher and lecturer followed, culminating with a post at the prestigious London University Institute of Education. Dorothy's personal health journey took her to homeopathy, and she developed her knowledge and love of homeopathic remedies while bringing up her family. Inspired to train as a homeopath, she has found a career which combines her love of puzzles and patterns with the focus on individuals. She has a thriving practice and is passionate about empowering people to take control of their own everyday health issues using self-help homeopathy.

Dorothy's Secrets

When I was 19, my partner and I won a race to hitchhike three-legged as far as possible in 24 hours. We got all the way from Cambridge to the Scottish Highlands!

In the middle of summer some friends and I got up at 4.30 a.m. to listen to the birds singing their dawn chorus then we sang back to the birds – a magical experience.

As a member of the Royal Liverpool Philharmonic Choir I worked with Paul McCartney on the world premiere of his Liverpool Oratorio.

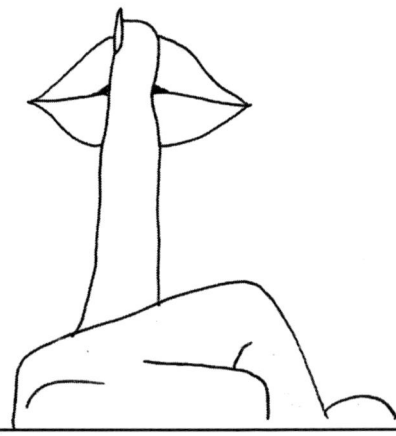

The Miracle Tree

The walk up the road had never seemed so long: step by exhausted step I dragged myself along. I'd felt so unwell for so long: I'd been off work for six weeks with the worst headache and absolutely no appetite or energy to do anything. This felt like the most important journey I'd ever made, and I had to get there in the next five minutes to stand a chance of seeing someone – anyone – to make me feel better. And so I ended up knocking on the door of a doctor I hadn't seen before, and I started to tell the story I'd told many times before, about my sinus infection which went away when I had antibiotics but which came straight back as soon as I stopped taking them. I wondered if I might be allergic to the tree growing outside my bedroom window.

"What's the tree?" he asked. That wasn't a question I'd been asked before! Luckily, I'd looked it up because I was interested in trees. "It's a Thuja occidentalis." And then his eyes lit up. This wasn't going like a standard doctor's consultation, and I was just about to find out why.

"You may or may not know" he said, "That I'm a homeopath as well as a doctor."

"What on earth is a homeopath?" I thought.

"Homeopaths have a remedy made from that tree," he continued, and he reached up and took down a thick green book. This is where it got really strange; he opened the book to "Thuja" and read out *my exact sinus symptoms! Exactly what I'd been struggling with for months!*

"Yes, that's it!" I said, "how did you know what it was like?"

"Well I can give you two choices, either try the homeopathic remedy which matches your symptoms, though I can't guarantee success, or have some more antibiotics."

Well the antibiotics had never helped for long so what did I have to lose by trying the homeopathic remedy, whatever THAT might be? So I picked up my prescription for three pills of Thuja 200C, one to be taken after each meal on a particular day. I'd always trusted doctors and followed their advice to the letter, so I trusted this homeopathic doctor, even though I had no idea what he was talking about. He seemed to be offering something more tailor-made, something which matched my particular symptoms, and I was tired of being tired – I needed my life back. So when I picked up my prescription and it was literally three little white pills I suspended my disbelief, took them home and started taking them the very next day.

And here's what happened: I took the three pills and forgot about it. Nothing changed immediately, but I gradually became aware of something dripping down the back of my throat, and a few days after that I realised my headache had gone. My sinuses had gently and effectively cleared themselves. The really magic thing is, unlike with all the different antibiotics I'd had, the infection didn't come straight back when I stopped taking them! I felt better than I had in months and didn't care how it had happened, I was just relieved to be feeling better at last.

To say I was impressed was an understatement. How had these homeopathic remedies effectively jolted my sinuses out of infection mode and reset them to being healthy? My body seemed to be giving me a clear message that this persistent and debilitating but relatively minor health niggle had been resolved using this different approach.

This got me thinking, and I'm going to condense years of evolving thoughts into a couple of paragraphs. What was so different about the homeopathic remedies that meant I didn't get sick again as soon as I stopped taking them? The antibiotics were fighting the infection in my sinuses, taking away the germs and making me feel better, but my body was still weak and depleted so as soon as the antibiotics stopped killing the germs the germs came back! The homeopathic remedy, on the other hand, was working with the underlying imbalance in my body – the reason *why* the infections kept coming back, so the next time the germs came along my body wasn't as weak and defenceless and the germs couldn't manage to invade. That's a huge difference in approach!

For the first time I started to wonder whether my symptoms were a signal that something was causing my body to get out of balance. By addressing the imbalance my body was able to mend. By just killing the infection my body rapidly became sick again, because the imbalance was still there. This was mind blowing! Think about it: in our society we tend to accept that once we get sick, we stay sick and need drugs to keep us comfortable. I'd discovered something which did the opposite – quickly and painlessly made me better. Full stop better – symptoms gone, no more problem.

It seems to me to be so much more effective to treat the underlying imbalance, yet Western medicine takes a different approach, and all our government-sponsored healthcare systems follow Western medicine. Why? If we truly want people to be healthy rather than sick, surely we as a society would want to focus on rebalancing our bodies rather than handing out quick fixes which make people feel better without addressing the root causes of illness? Not to mention the difference in cost – homeopathic sugar pills are SO much cheaper than pharmaceutical drugs.

Now don't get me wrong, I'm not saying Western medicine has no uses – it's ability to save lives in an emergency is unequalled. But most of the time we go to the doctor for something pretty trivial which isn't going to kill us. We look to doctors to make us better, yet let's flash back to my poor infected sinuses and the course after course of expensive antibiotics I received; with hindsight the many doctors I saw were doing their best with the training they'd received, but I was just being made to FEEL better rather than BE better.

Somehow the homeopathy got to the root cause of my issue and the problem was resolved. Now maybe the 'somehow' is part of the problem – no-one can currently explain how homeopathy works. That doesn't mean, though, that it doesn't work, it just means we don't know. As a society we're very obsessed with 'science' and it having all the answers. I've got a science degree and I understand what science is really about – enquiry, it's about finding out more about the world around us. Each little experiment adds a tiny bit to the sum of knowledge about our world. Yet there's a tendency to think that if we can't explain something it's unscientific and wrong. Actually, that viewpoint is what's unscientific and wrong! If something can't be explained a good scientist will carry out a lot of observations in order to find out more about something.

Now let's fast forward 30 years. I'm a busy and successful homeopath working with clients who have all sorts of issues they'd like support with, and they're all at different stages in their personal health journey. Some of them have seen homeopaths before, some can vaguely remember being taken along to see someone in their childhood, and some are at their wit's end having taken prescription drugs non-stop for years and are feeling gradually worse rather than better, some buy into there being a cause within their body for their discomfort. And then this morning I was talking to a prospective client who told me about her sinuses, how she regularly has twelve lots of antibiotics in a single year and often three courses back-to-back. After the call ended, I suddenly saw myself struggling, exhausted along the road, desperate to have my life back, and realised how far on my journey I'd come and how grateful I was for that tree outside my bedroom window. Without that Thuja tree I wouldn't have been so unwell, I wouldn't have taken a punt on something I'd never heard of but which just had to be worth a try, and I wouldn't have found my fulfilling career.

Listen to your body: if you're in pain it's trying to tell you something needs to change.

Dorothy Watt

Grow and Reflect with Dorothy

Isn't it strange how we learn to do the same as everyone else? From when we're very young there's a right way to do things and everything else is wrong. And as time goes on, we're conditioned to do more things the right way. In terms of our health this conditioning starts before we're born, at the moment our mother becomes pregnant and goes to the doctor to be monitored through the pregnancy; it's not surprising the conditioning runs so deep!

But there is more, there is another way of thinking about health and wellness which requires us to take responsibility for our own health rather than hand that responsibility over to doctors who are trained to make us *feel* better rather than *be* better.

Does this resonate with you? Maybe you're stuck in this difficult situation where you have uncomfortable symptoms you'd rather not have, drugs you'd rather not be taking and life you're not fully embracing. Does the idea of a deeper root cause for your ailments seem strangely attractive though unfamiliar? Are you ready to embark on a journey of self-discovery in order to free yourself from your pain? Read on! Now's your chance to explore more.

1. Sit comfortably and quietly for a few moments. Close your eyes and listen to your body. How does it feel? Is there any pain or discomfort? Where is that?

2. Did you always have this discomfort? Think back to a time when it wasn't there. How does it feel not having that familiar discomfort?

3. If you didn't always have that discomfort or pain maybe you don't need to have it in the future! Can you think of anything which happened in your life around the time the discomfort started? Have you got any emotions beginning to surface?

This process I've invited you to experience shows you the approach I take as a homeopath when I support you to release your pain gradually and gently. Except when you work with me, it's easier than what you've just done because you'll be taking your bespoke homeopathic remedies which have been specially chosen to match your symptoms. These remedies will provide your body with the support to let go of stored emotions and therefore pain so you can focus your energy on moving forwards with your life. Many clients report they feel lighter and more alive than they remember being for some time, just like I did after my first ever remedies.

If you'd like to take some responsibility for your own health follow the link below and download my guide to the absolute essential homeopathic products to keep in your kitchen cupboard.

www.dorothywatt.com/4-homeopathic-must-haves-for-your-kitchen-cupboard-2/

With these products you can learn to deal with annoying day-to-day ailments in a way which helps you recover more quickly and easily. And, by signing up to my mailing list, you'll learn more about me and be first to know about my new blogs and homeopathic tips..

CONTACT DOROTHY

www.youtube.com/channel/
UCv6IXGNMTvR1L2jLqpWxYqA

www.linkedin.com/in/dorothy-watt-holistic-
wellness-advocate-8919b18b/

www.dorothywatt.com

www.dorothywatt.com/work-with-me/
workshop-courses for 20% off

Space for your thoughts ...

....

....

....

....

....

....

....

....

....

....

....

....

....

....

....

....

....

....

I am a woman who lives life to the fullest.

JULIE MAIGRET SHAPIRO

Julie founded Women Who Stay in the Game to inspire midlife women to find their purpose and share their unique gifts with the world.

Julie works with women who are feeling marginalized, unfulfilled and meant for bigger things. She helps women rediscover their passion and create more fulfilling lives.

Julie worked as a learning and development leader at the University of California, Berkeley. She holds a BA from UC Berkeley and a master's degree from Middlebury College. She is a certified executive coach from the Berkeley Executive Coaching Institute.

Julie lives in Berkeley, California. She loves travel and has lived in Italy, France and Spain and is fluent in Italian, French and Spanish.

Julie's Secrets

I can read your fortune in a cup of Turkish coffee.

My superpower is finding the right gift and card for every occasion.

I love to travel internationally. My happiest moment was swimming in the Aegean.

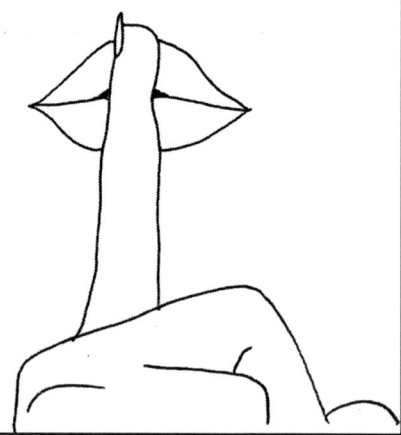

Lost and Found
The Missing Piece

The moment I logged onto Zoom for my weekly one-on-one meeting with my sales manager, I realized that something was off. There were three people on the call: my manager, the head of HR and the CEO. Feeling vulnerable, I tried to excuse myself. "Oh sorry! I must be early. I'll join later," I said, starting to log off when they all cried "No wait!"

I froze. I knew then that my 12-year career was about to abruptly end. The head of HR started explaining that due to the Covid-19 pandemic, they had to lay people off. I felt sick to my stomach.

As my managers were breaking the news, I saw their mouths moving, but I couldn't hear anything. I was lost in my own thoughts. I loved my job, and I was one of the top performers! Why would they get rid of *me*? My heart was pounding, and I couldn't look at any of them. All I could see were my own terrified eyes staring back at me from my Zoom image.

My thoughts were racing: What will become of me now? How will I be able to afford to live in the Bay Area? Who will hire me during a pandemic? What about my reputation? I wasn't going to let them see me cry. I made it through the call. Once it ended, I threw myself on my sofa

ng my job felt like losing my identity. Who
he role I had learned to play so well?

ed back to when my mother died nine
carmer. As her only child, I was my mother's
caregiver for several years before she passed away. It had
been painful to see her health decline and overwhelming
to take care of her while working at a demanding job.
There was no other family member to help out, so I had to
manage her care on my own.

After losing her, my life felt empty. To deal with the pain, I
buried myself in my work. My job in business development
was all-encompassing. I worked with international clients
around the clock and traveled all over the world. There
was always a new deal to pursue. Perpetually busy and on
the go – I had no idle time.

Between losing my mother and my job, I felt as if my
former life had evaporated. I had nothing left to anchor me.
All I could feel was the shame of losing my job. I felt like
damaged goods. After several days of despair, I mustered
the courage to share what had happened with a few trusted
friends. The weight of my shame started to lift. Although
I loved my job, I had often thought of making a change. I
longed to learn new things and advance in my career.

With Covid-19 everything seemed to stand still. My only
companion at home was my fifteen-and-a-half-year-old
Pomeranian, Bailey. When my job ended, I felt lost without
a busy schedule to define my days. Once I came to terms
with my situation and let go of my shame, I realized that
this was a new beginning for me. I had the gift of time: I
could fill my days as I wished!

It had been more than a decade since I had the space to think about my own wants and needs. I now had the opportunity to get to know the Julie I had long forgotten. Who was she? What did she desire?

I began to relish my freedom and time alone. It felt as if I were on an adventure. Little by little, I started living in the moment. I rediscovered my *joie de vivre* by reconnecting with my curiosity, sense of humor and playfulness. I felt alive.

For the longest time, I had dreamt of being a writer. Inspired to dive in, I signed up for a writing class and joined a community of aspiring writers. My creativity began to soar. I even had an idea for a book.

Around the same time, I took a career values assessment to help me determine what values are most important to me. The results of the assessment surprised me. Discovering that creativity was my driving force was unexpected and thrilling. The assessment affirmed that I was on the right path and motivated me to explore this new identity.

Although my lifelong dream was to write, I didn't think it was possible for me. As a child, I was full of creativity, I took acting, singing, art, music and dance lessons. I wrote stories.

In college, I enrolled in a creative writing class to pursue my dream. Unfortunately, soon after, my inner critic got the best of me. I started comparing myself to the other students in my class and believed that everyone else was more talented than me. I dropped the class, convinced that writing wasn't in the cards for me. My mother had always said I wrote beautifully. But she was my mother.

In the fall of 2021, a woman from my writing group reached out to me. She had recently become a publisher and was putting together a multi-author book. She asked me if I wanted to write a story for her upcoming book, *Authentic*. I couldn't believe she was asking *me*! It felt like an incredible opportunity. I would become a published author!

Being asked to write a story felt like a sign to keep going. Despite my trepidation about whether I could pull it off, I said yes. When I began to write my story, I found it very difficult. All of my self-critical, perfectionistic tendencies reappeared making it challenging for me to write from my heart. I told the publisher about my struggles, and she insisted that I had a story worth telling and convinced me to continue. Reassured, I persevered.

A requirement for participating in the multi-author book was to promote the book launch to my network on social media. I was used to promoting professors and making their work more visible, yet felt shy about showcasing my own work. Nevertheless, I was determined to do it.

I realized that throughout my career, I had stayed in the background – hiding out. I never felt as if I could take center stage, even though I desperately wanted to. That was the old me. This time I chose to use my voice and share my words. I knew it was my moment to do so.

Completing my chapter and having it published was exhilarating! I felt inspired to continue writing. For the first time, I felt seen, heard and in charge of my destiny. I no longer was defined by a role. Instead, I was defined by how I showed up in the world. I had shown up courageously and it was liberating.

Inspired by what felt like a huge transformation, I decided to start my own coaching business to help women like me deal with life transitions. I created *Women Who Stay in the Game* for women who are stuck, lost, or uninspired and feel called to make a difference in the world. My mission is to help midlife women find their passion, purpose and build a fulfilling life.

My first business challenge was learning how to write powerful social media posts to attract clients. Given my reticent nature, this did not come naturally. Luckily, I saw a post from Debora Luzi offering a three-day workshop on social media writing and I signed up.

All the pieces of the puzzle have come together. I joined Debora's Writing Academy and have learned to show up authentically and create compelling content that boosts my online presence. Within the Writing Academy, I met the most supportive community of women entrepreneurs. I learn so much from each of them every day. I have truly found my tribe! These women are dedicated to helping others by sharing their gifts and they inspire me to do the same.

Creating my own venture is exciting for me. It is a powerful experience to help other women regain their confidence and I am loving every minute of it. For the first time, I am owning my voice and sharing my unique point of view with others.

Showing up authentically has been life-changing. I'm enjoying more visibility and people are responding to my enthusiasm. I am getting offers to speak at conferences, to be on podcasts, to teach, and I am saying "yes!"

I now see that losing my job and my long-held career identity gave me the space I needed to rediscover my innate gifts. The many new people and experiences that have come into my life since that fateful Zoom call have guided me step-by-step to trust myself and the journey I am on. They have helped me navigate the unknown and embrace my new identity as a creative person, a writer and an entrepreneur.

When you feel knocked down by life, remember that you have an opportunity to try something new. Your life is rich with possibilities. Choose to make it a great one!

Julie Maigret Shapiro

Grow and Reflect with Julie

As a child, I spent hours alone drawing, painting, writing stories and playing. I lived in my imagination and my life was filled with magical inspiration. I never questioned my ability to draw, write, etc. I just let myself be in the moment. I created for the pure pleasure of self-expression. You can see in the picture below that I was completely absorbed in the flow of the moment. Creativity was a part of me.

In middle school, I noticed that other children could draw better than me and my self-consciousness kicked in. It was no longer enough to feel joy from my self-expression. Now, I had to be *good* at drawing, painting etc. Once I began to compare myself to others, my inner critic was born. I worried that I wasn't talented enough to draw. From that point on my perfectionist self only allowed me to attempt things I knew I would be successful at doing. Avoiding failure at all costs made my list of creative pursuits markedly shorter.

Having overcome the need to be perfect, I now enjoy a mix of pure self-expression and projects that I want to share with others. As part of my new identity, I embrace different perspectives and creativity without a specific agenda. I no longer let the possibility of failure deter me. I haven't completely ditched my inner critic, but I have learned how to work with her.

Writing Prompts:

Trying on a new identity can give us the courage to do things we might not normally do.

Let's take a journey back to your childhood to reconnect with the younger you. This will remind you of what was important to you as a child.

Are there any childhood dreams that still have a place in your heart?

1. Choose a childhood photo of yourself that moves you.

   - What do you like about the photo?
   - What memories/feelings does it evoke?
   - Consider talking to family members to get more information about the younger you.

2. Think about your childhood. *w/ doll house*
    - How did you like to spend your time?
    - What made you laugh? *?*
    - What was your big dream for when you grew up?

Social Worker @ School

help
Kids
families
· coach
grad

3. Next, we are going to use our imagination.

- I want you to choose an identity that lights you up. Then you are going to try on this new identity by dressing up, as you imagine they would, and acting as if this is the new you.

  - What is different about your energy?
  - The way you speak? *w/ confidence,*
  - The way you behave? *ext*

- *in charge, authent* Now, go someplace where the *new you* would ✗ hang out. *University*

- Make sure to interact with others as the *new you!*

- I encourage you to stay open to possibilities and set aside any preconceptions.

- Have fun with it!

4. Reflection time ... Journal about what your experience was like taking on this new persona. There is space over the page to do this.

- How did you feel as this person? *Me,*

- Can you describe what was different about you?

- What did you learn from this experience?

- What qualities or activities would you like to bring into your life from this experience?

- What steps can you take to incorporate some of the *new you* into your life?

Julie Maigret Shapiro as a child

My Gift to you: My 4-Step Process To Creating The Career
Of Your Dreams:
www.womenwhostayinthegame.com/Gift

CONTACT JULIE

www.facebook.com/people/Julie-Shapiro/100009067917268/

www.linkedin.com/in/juliejmshapiro/

www.womenwhostayinthegame.com

www.womenwhostayinthegame.com/Gift/

Space for your thoughts ...

....

....

....

....

....

....

....

....

....

....

....

....

....

....

....

....

....

....

....

I am a woman who dares to be confident, a catalyst for life and business transformation.

LUCIA MARGARIDA PESTANA

Lucia Margarida Pestana is a catalyst for life and business transformation.

In the past ten years, she built a very successful career as a human resources professional, she has been labelled a trailblazer in the industry for her contribution to employee engagement and as an advocate for Investors in People.

After being made redundant in 2020, she enrolled on the biggest adventure of her life as the proud owner of Pestana's HR and Coaching. Lucia is a 'multipotentialite' who embraces many different roles, including HR consulting, business development, career coaching, and support coaching.

Her career is not what defines Lucia; her charismatic nature, kindness and ability to listen and provide perspective in hardship are! A problem shared is a problem solved is one of her mottos.

Being a woman who dares to desire, Lucia is continually growing and developing and thoroughly enjoys sharing her journey with like-minded women; she has dared the stage at The Women Who Dare to Desire Conference in 2020 and created Pu$$y Portal Sisterhood Circle, a sacred place for women to gather and heal.

Lucia's Secrets

Lucia's entrepreneur and leadership journey started at the age of 14 when she and her friends co-founded New Generation an entertainment group for the local community. They are still going today.

She is an adventurer who loves to give back; She has abseiled, slept in the cold, boxed, and Aussie rappelled to raise over £5000 for charity.

When Lucia was seventeen, She found that her first career passion was radio broadcasting. She interviewed two famous Portuguese bands and participated in a national competition for Young Radio Broadcasters.

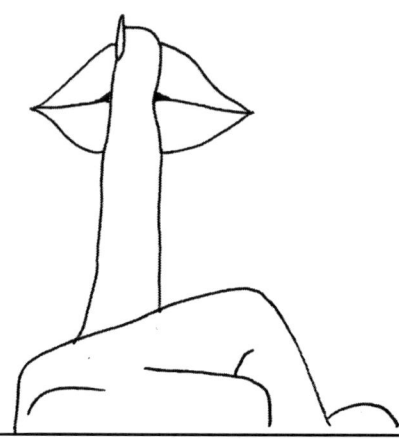

The Gift from the Tooth Fairy

As I sit on the floor of my room, packing all the belongings I have accumulated over the years, I feel pretty nostalgic.

So many things, do I really need all of them?

Moving is not something I enjoy, and I am honestly quite proud that since moving to the UK 24 years ago, I have only moved five times; this is my sixth move, I am ready for a new chapter in my life and cannot wait to get going.

I have never felt so confident or reassured as I do now! I feel so ready for this change, and I welcome another chapter for the woman who dares and lives by it.

As I see all the boxes starting to pile up in the living room, I wonder, do I need all these things? Each box is filled with many memories, of places and times that contributed to my growth.

As I started packing all my photos and papers, a promo design I had created just fell out, and it took me on a trip down memory lane.

I created it in 2014, the year that tested me to my core, when seeing my health on the line really challenged me to look within. It was not the easiest year; I don't think I have ever felt so brave and so lost simultaneously.

I started the year burying my aunt after she lost her battle with cancer, then it was my own health on the line.

Hospital waiting areas became my thinking ground; it was a long year waiting to figure out what was happening with me and my body. I kept going, and I was strong, yet I was all alone, I could not bear to share what was going on inside me as I could not deal with anyone's pity.

I had many sleepless nights wondering what was wrong, until I got a confirmed diagnosis of coeliac disease and a benign tumour. This was topped up with invasive dental treatment. Sadness engulfed my mind, I always felt I needed to carry the burden of the world on my shoulders and would not dare to share mine; on the one hand, it was strength, on the other, it invited loneliness.

When I found this promo design, a raffle prize draw for my "smile journey," I felt proud to see how far I had come.

I remember the day I dared to speak up and say exactly how it felt about my crooked smile, how self-conscious I was, and how I thought I was not beautiful, I was not confident and how I felt ugly.

The truth was that I was always confident, and everyone could see that; even though I was too shy to admit it, I knew I was confident too.

Back then I didn't realise how lucky I was, I needed invasive dental implant treatment to correct my protruding teeth and give me a beautiful smile.

The moment I dared to speak up and admit it to myself and my friend is when everything changed. At that moment I allowed myself to be held and supported by my dearest friend Debora. She went through leaps and bounds to find the best dentist to give me my beautiful smile.

For the first time in a long time, I allowed someone to help me, she booked my first appointment, took time out of work to go with me, and literally held my hand when we walked through and I sat in the dentist's chair. I was petrified by dentists.

It also started an even bigger battle inside me; at the time, I thought that if I fixed my smile, I would be more confident, I would feel beautiful and then I would be loved more.

That could not be further from the truth because confidence doesn't come from your external appearance or the material things you accumulate. It comes from your core.

With confidence comes resilience. I didn't have the money for all my treatment, this was a time of hardship because I had a bigger vision and was creative with the different ways to raise money the prize draw was a great idea.

In the past, I would have been terrified and ashamed of asking people for money, yet my vision was so big that I had to overcome this shame. I did raffle prize draws, I sold old clothes and jewellery at car boot sales and I created a GoFundMe page.

People cyberbullied me for creating a page and asking for money, they could not believe that as a successful manager I should be doing it, which could have shattered my confidence, but they failed, I am not going to pretend it did not affect me, it did upset me, and I thought this person is hurting because they would not dare to do what I have done.

No matter what I needed to do, I would do it because my vision and my desire for a beautiful smile was bigger than anything else.

A problem shared is a problem solved

LUCIA MARGARIDA PESTANA

My confidence was unshattered because it came from this conviction in my core, it taught me to ask for help, and it taught me that I didn't need to always be the giver.

That core confidence helped me raise over £23K to pay all my medical expenses, I let go of shame, healed emotionally, and made long-lasting friendships.

The financial support was a nice thing to have but nothing compared to the feeling of gratitude and love I received from everyone who supported me on this journey.

That is why I always say a problem shared is a problem solved!

It took me so long to realise that I could do anything. I enjoy putting on my favourite makeup and a killer outfit. It makes me feel good.

However, nothing will match up to the unshakable confidence that is in my core and makes me stand tall in my divine feminine power.

I didn't know I had that kind of strength within me until I needed to step up and create that change in my life.

Confidence is sexy; many people in my life have said I am confident and some have felt intimidated by it because they know the power it holds.

People still ask me today why I spent so much money on my teeth when I could buy a house?

My answer is simple: I don't want to accumulate more things in my life, I want to look after myself, and my health is way more important than buying a house.

Why did I think going through a painful process would make me more confident?

Honestly, like many, I was brainwashed with text, magazines, movies and products that sold confidence. The media always painted a picture that you need to be skinny to be confident or that you need to wear a suit to be confident. That could not be further from the truth.

I can firmly say that confidence comes from your core. Just imagine an apple; is an apple confident?

In my eyes, yes, because when you reach its core, you reject the seeds; the seeds, on the other hand, don't care. They are confident they will be going to the ground and flourish once again as an apple tree and hopefully be able to grow into an orchard.

An apple's mission is not to be liked, or to be anything else; having that core belief in itself, is what confidence is about.

With confidence comes fearlessness. When you draw from your core confidence, you are unstoppable, nothing is an obstacle, and everything is an opportunity.

Was I always this strong and confident?

Yes, I always knew deep down that I was destined to be and achieve great things at my core!

And so are you!

Be fearless, be grateful, be core confident. It is so sexy.

Lucia Margarida Pestana

Grow and Reflect with Lucia

Do you remember when you were a child? How adventurous were you? Were you afraid of jumping in at any fun opportunity, or did you ask how high you needed to jump?

Fear was non-existent for me, and it has made me land in a few sticky situations which I always managed to get myself out of, miraculously unscraped.

Can I let you into a little secret? That child I used to be is still inside of me and is inside of you too.

Let's travel back to a time and space where you wore your heart on your sleeve, where a no from your parents meant a yes in your mind, and where you dared to experience every fun and adventurous opportunity that presented itself to you.

Are the corners of your lips going upwards, rejoicing in this beautiful memory of how fun and carefree you used to be? Where is that person now?

Take a deep breath before you answer and remember that person is still very much alive within you. You may have been programmed by society to be more this or more that so that you blend in and become nothing more than just a number.

Is that the real you?

Do you wish to be more confident?

Here is how you can do it:

Step One

Strip back all the accessories you feel make you confident, for example, clothes, job, car, strip back everything. Focus on your core, the place where you feel butterflies, the pit of your stomach, and bring back that innocence and curiosity where everything is a possibility.

Stay with those feelings, don't pass any judgment. This is the place where your core confidence lies. It is within you.

Step Two

Forget other people's opinions of you; if someone is building you up, you know you've found your Debora, who will hold your hand in the most challenging moments and the happiest because you know you have a friend for life.

If they bring you down, stay as far away as possible because these people's mission in life is to wallow in self pity.

Step Three

Core confidence is conviction, not arrogance, be firm in your expression and be fair. Don't allow this power to go to your head. Keep your heart open and show love.

Step Four

Embody your core confidence in everything you do, from running your business to pursuing your desires; take this strength with you and be the incredible daring woman you were born to be!

You were not born to be just a number, a person who walks because they see other people walking. You are a person who is meant to stand out from the crowd.

Because you are reading this book, you are a Person Who Dares to Desire. It is time to bring that fierce leader within you and allow it to soar. Unleash that powerful adventurer within you, where no opportunity is left on the table.

Let your core confidence shine; it is who you are inside and out, a flame that can never be extinguished unless you allow it to.

Now grab a pen and start reconnecting with your core confidence. I will guide you with the questions below to bring your core confidence into centre stage and allow it to guide you in your life and business.

* Pick up a mirror and bring it close to your eyes (5 cms or so), look deep within your eyes, the gateway to your soul, and ask this question: Where is that carefree person? Where is that person who believed everything is possible? Invite them to come out and play.

    Journal on the following page whatever comes up for you.

Where is that carefree person?

★ What fears are rising when you journalled on the above questions? Now write for yourself ten affirmations that will counteract your fears. For example, "I am core confident!" "I show up confidently in every situation."

1. ....

2. ....

3. ....

4. ....

5. ....

6. ....

7. ....

8. ....

9. ....

10. ....

✱ Now DARE to show up with your core confidence, declare it to the world, reintroduce yourself, let the world know how magnetic and powerful you are if you are willing to stretch yourself. Why don't you post a video declaring your power?

My gift to you: Pussy Portal Sisterhood Circle is my proudest creation and a haven for all women who dare to desire. Attend one of the events for free:

https://pestanashrandcoaching.ck.page/7d62f537ff

CONTACT LUCIA

www.linkedin.com/in/lucia-margarida-pestana-cipdassociate/

www.instagram.com/luciapestanaofficial/

www.pestanashrandcoaching.com

www.pestanashrandcoaching.ck.page/7d62f537ff

Space for your thoughts ...

....

....

....

....

....

....

....

....

....

....

....

....

....

....

....

....

....

....

I am a woman who spreads beauty wherever I go.

LOREDANA THOENIG

Romanian born, Greek in her heart, living in Spain, Loredana is a certified Women's Empowerment Coach and founder of FiloGynia® (a successful brand of natural supplements for women).

As an Empowerment Coach and Female Wellbeing Mentor, Loredana helps women of the modern world reconnect with their intrinsic nature, cultivate wisdom, inner beauty, and outer radiance to thrive living in congruence with who they really are.

For her, beauty is a spiritual gift given to all girls at birth, a spark that aspires to be awakened to fully shine and freely express itself throughout every woman on Earth. Loredana lives for the purpose of turning on the Goddess energy within every woman who desires to fully embody her wise and sexy feminine soul.

Expert in feminine holistic self-care, Loredana efficiently blends her expertise as a former fashion model, her wisdom as an Holistic Childbirth Educator with coaching to infuse her own empowerment method: *Embody your Feminine*

Greatness. Her passion is to see women thriving while living sexy lives. She simply loves seeing women shine from the inside out when they let go of the inner misogynist and reconnect with the natural parts of themselves.

Women come to her feeling lost, exhausted, insecure, invisible, disconnected from their sensuality and wisdom, to eventually awaken and embody their most irresistible and confident feminine selves.

Loredana's secrets

I have lived in four different countries, and I speak five languages and understand seven. My favourite place on earth is Greece. I lived in Athens for two years ('97 to '99) and after so many years I still speak, read and write Greek. I visit Greece every year and I desire to organise goddess retreats over there.

In 2008, after the homebirth of my daughter and after reading Dr Joe Dispenza's work, I experienced a major self-healing which led me to study and understand the science behind transformation. Neuroscience and quantum physics have become my passion. I healed my hearing through meditation, and I became one of Dr Joe's advanced students and a team leader. (My testimonial is here: https://youtu.be/XLpwo53CXMM)

At 16, the age when goddess Aphrodite emerges in every girl, with all her magnificent attributes: beauty, femininity, sensuality, love, I was chosen as a finalist in the national beauty contest, Miss Teen, from among 850 beautiful teen girls.

Embodying the power of feminine nature

Somehow, I've always felt that within my body resides an infinite fountain of creativity, vitality, beauty, wellbeing and absolute delight. I was about six years old when I began to sense the goddess within me, but it took me years to listen to her voice and let her guide me with full trust in a world that strives to repress her.

The Eastern European country I was born and grew up in, Romania, is known for the story of Dracula but is also famous for the exquisite beauty of its women. Most of them cultivate their femininity not only in their outer appearance but also by taking good care of their vital energy in natural ways. Nature, potions and infusions made from plants, women's gatherings, journaling and love rituals were all part of the feminine traditions in my family and community.

I grew up being and feeling fully alive in my body and I have had a very special fascination with women's beauty since I was a little girl. I dreamed of becoming a fashion model and when the communist dictatorship ended, I took my chance.

At 19 I left my family and my country and emigrated to Greece. I was so happy to be admitted to one of the best modelling agencies in Athens. I could finally be free to be me as I was living my soul's biggest desire. Life in Athens was exotic. The place where Goddesses were born.

I felt free and energized but, to my big surprise I also encountered there a huge resistance, discrimination, and racism towards Eastern European women.

I worked so hard to sustain myself financially and help my family back home but that was nothing compared to the efforts I made in keeping my self-esteem intact every time a client offended me or decided to pay me less, just because I was Romanian. It wasn't easy at all, but with the help of wonderful people, within one year I spoke the language perfectly, studied Greek culture and had become a very successful model.

Two years later I left my Greek career and went to Paris. It was the place where I flourished and prospered both personally and professionally. In that jungle of fashion, despite the fact that I didn't fulfil the strict requirements for physical shape and size that professional models "must have", I found a way to succeed. I loved fashion and that was my moment. I had no time to blame, complain or compare myself with other models. Instead, I focussed my efforts on developing a charismatic personality, practicing self-confidence, and cultivating total self-care which resulted in embodying a feminine presence that fashion professionals adored.

I was thriving in my body and flourishing in my unapologetic feminine expression when, a year later, I decided to move to Barcelona. Right after moving to Spain, I changed fashion for acting and got married to a handsome and successful businessman. Immediately after the wedding we decided to have a baby.

On a rainy summer day in 2004, at age 28, I became a mother for the first time. The happiness of having my baby in my arms was shivering throughout my body. I desired to have a natural birth in one of the best private clinics in town. Before that day, I'd never been hospitalised. My cultural tradition of using nature's medicine while growing up in Romania, and the trust and vitality I felt in my body, gave me the confidence that I was in possession of the power to give birth without interferences.

As I went through such a relaxed and wonderful pregnancy, I trusted that everything would go fine.

But once at the clinic, I found myself immersed in a series of protocols and unnecessary interventions that went against everything I had trusted until then. The healthcare team, starting with the midwife who broke my waters without asking my permission, and the doctor who anaesthetised my belly, to the nurses who separated me from my baby after birth, made me feel completely robbed of my power, violated and ignored in my needs and rights.

I felt so impotent and traumatized by a system that disabled me as a mother and as a woman. That disempowering feeling, that neither my body nor my sexuality nor my baby belonged to me, was rising in my being and impregnated every corner of my feminine soul.

Away from my roots, away from home without my mother or any mother figure to nourish me, I felt alone, lost and frightened during the whole postpartum phase. I was new in Spain and had no community to support me as a new mother. Because of the way they treated my body, my womb and my baby in the hospital during the birthing process, my energy turned off completely and I consequently suffered exhaustion, lack of libido, lack of creativity, anxiety and even depressive states. I didn't feel good in my body anymore. I was young and good looking, and I had my before-pregnancy figure, but I wasn't feeling attractive anymore. Where did my aliveness go?

My life looked perfect on the outside, but deep within I had a constant feeling of dissatisfaction, and the worst was that I was afraid to confess it. I was in a profound crisis, and I had no idea what was happening. All I knew was that I needed to find a way to come back to that inner feeling of joy and sensuality. I wanted to feel good in my body. I wanted to feel like a woman again.

I looked for solutions everywhere. I became a junkie of spirituality, self-development, therapy and psychology. I studied childbirth education, became a birth doula and worked with pregnant women. Through empowering and giving support to new mothers, I was healing and mothering myself. I went to different experts in tantra and I began my studies in psychology, energy healing and neuroscience.

I learned a lot about female physiology and how a woman's body works. To heal and thrive, I had to retrain my body to feel safe, relaxed, and open again.

During the childbirth education classes I took with the prestigious Dr Michele Odent, I learned that the cocktail of feminine hormones of pleasure, which the body releases during birth and lactation, are the same that women's bodies release during lovemaking. This chemistry that softens and opens the female body for birth or intimacy needs special conditions to flow. I understood that the frenetic rhythm of our modern world, or the cold medical system blocks the release of the wellbeing hormones in women. When we don't feel safe, our feminine energy shrinks, and the body becomes tense. That explained why my body shut down for so long.

During those years all I did was explore, study and learn powerful practices that help the female body relax into full trust.

The desire to have a second child filled my heart. But this time I said, "I'll do it my way". During this pregnancy I kept practicing body awareness and connection with my natural instincts and my in-womb daughter. I also chose to have a natural homebirth.

When the day came, I was amazed how fast my body opened, allowing my beautiful baby girl to smoothly come out. My body's vertical position helped me to remain relaxed and in absolute bliss. Surrounded and sustained by my wise midwife, Sofia, and two other women, I gave birth like a real powerful goddess.

I felt safe, as my body worked perfectly releasing the pleasure-hormonal cocktail it needed. What an orgasmic, ecstatic moment! I felt one with divinity and I trusted myself completely. The moment I had my sweet daughter in my arms and looked in her pure eyes, I understood that the female body was the sacred portal that brings Spirit into flesh.

Since then, I have felt the great power that arose from my womb like a volcano. I felt capable of anything, with a feeling of being home. I felt full, satisfied, happy and my life was completely transformed.

I was giving myself full attention and care as I was feeding my baby and taking care of my older son, surrounded by women who took care of me.

My midwife helped me recover fast with natural plant infusions. Different wise women made homemade formulas for me that helped me increase my energy, have the breast milk flow and lose the extra weight fast. Surrounded by so much love, my thoughts went to all the mothers who might go through difficult times. I must do something to help other women thrive, I thought.

The following years, I continued my studies. I joined world organisations for prenatal education and did a lot of humanitarian work helping young mothers with no resources.

Following the wisdom of my inner goddess energy, I deepened my studies in empowerment coaching and continued transforming women's lives. I listened to hundreds of women from all over the world and realised that women everywhere have common challenges and common desires. I saw too many women living disconnected from their bodies, feeling empty, lost and turned off while adapting to a frenetic rhythm created by men, for men. The world is still an unsafe place for women to thrive in their feminine expression. Women everywhere repress and ignore their feminine needs when pursuing career goals or taking care of others.

To thrive and prosper, we women need to have our vitality and aliveness turned on and come back into balance following our natural rhythm. We need to let go of that inner misogynist and honour our feminine nature. We need to take time for ourselves and refill our containers before serving others and we also need to be taken good care of by our communities.

That's why, over the past few years, I have used all my wisdom and finally launched my dream brand of natural supplements to give women the support they need to cultivate powerful feminine energy in their bodies and come back to balance.

Combining amazing ancestral herbal formulas with modern technology, I've created products that help women increase their feminine energy, beauty, health, and wellbeing. I basically amplified the mothering energy, so that every woman whose life I may touch can thrive in her feminine expression feeling supported and taken good care of.

Out of my love for Greek culture, I called the brand FiloGynia®, which means "Love for woman" (the complete opposite and antidote to misogyny) and I use it as a platform for educating and empowering women globally.

When you connect with your intrinsic nature and simply allow your feminine essence to shine through, you will be in awe of how powerful, magnetic and beautiful you truly are as a woman!

Loredana Thoenig

Grow and Reflect with Loredana

Dear Goddess,

If you live yearning to feel great in your fabulous female body and be happy with yourself but you don't know where to start, please allow me to be your guide for a while.

No matter of what's going on in your life right now, I want to remind you that you have the power to not only transform your life, but to expand and create entire universes. I want you to live grounded into the fullness of who you really are, because you deserve to live with inner plenitude and outer feminine splendour.

I would love to give you a glimpse of the energy you can awaken within when you let go of some false beliefs the world has instilled in you.

You'll see that when you dare to awaken and express your authentic feminine nature, your life completely transforms. Your relationships deepen, your inner and outer confidence is strengthened, your body shines, making you look and feel amazing as a whole, happy and irresistible woman.

Grab a pen and paper/journal (or write in the space provided) and sit in a quiet beautiful place. This is a moment for yourself. You don't need to take care of anyone. Stay fully present and eliminate anything that could distract you.

★ Can you remember the last time you felt amazing in your body? Who were you with? Where were you? How did you talk, walk, dress and treat yourself in general? Can you remember and describe the qualities you exuded when you were relaxed in your feminine essence?

★ Can you identify misogyny within you and in your life? How do you feel it goes against you staying true to your natural expression as a woman? What blocks your feminine radiance?

Do you have a belief (prejudice) about feminine women, or being feminine yourself? If yes, I invite you to explore how you learned that. Try this practice and see what happens: observe with whom and in which situations your energy flows and expands and in which it shrinks. In which situations do you feel you can be your true self, and in which do you feel repressed? Ask yourself how your life would be different if you'd fully trusted yourself and dared to fully express who you truly are as a woman.

★ To amplify your radiance and fearlessly shine, I invite you to find ways to cultivate, nourish and liberate your true feminine expression. Please never compare yourself to other women, because each one of us has a unique way to express femininity. Instead, make a list of the women you resonate with and what you admire in them. Embody greatness by practicing those qualities.

CONTACT LOREDANA

 www.facebook.com/YourFeminineNature

 www.linkedin.com/services/page/
a817b431367b86a7a3

 www.filogynia.com

www.filogynia.com/en/vitalyin
Discount code: VITALYIN15

Space for your thoughts ...

....

....

....

....

....

....

....

....

....

....

....

....

....

....

....

....

....

....

....

I am a woman who dares to desire, a woman who leads herself first and whose desires are bigger than her fears.

DEBORA LUZI

Debora Luzi is a word alchemist, author and speaker. She is the founder of the Writing Academy for Entrepreneurs, the only global elite community for entrepreneurs to learn how to turn their words into sales and fully own their voice and their mission. She is passionate about teaching women to show up fully in all their purest and most real magic, whatever that might look like. She is here to empower women to take centre stage and shine their light. Debora is also the founder of the Women Who Dare to Desire Global Conference, a centre stage for any woman, no matter what their background and speaking experience, to share their stories and inspire the world. Debora's approach to public speaking is unique and passionate. Her teachings are drawn from her own experience of acting and involve improvisations, emotional presence, stage presence and intuition.

Debora also regularly organises healing circles in London called The Soulful Writers' Healing Circle.

Debora strongly believes that the WORD is your OYSTER.

Debora's Secrets

I travelled as a backpacker to more than 55 countries, working in many of them to earn the money to reach the next one.

I swam with a huge whale shark in Utila, Honduras. The scuba instructor on the boat said to all the divers to wait before jumping in the waters as the whale shark was passing by, but I understood to jump, so I did and found myself swimming next to the animal.

When I was seventeen, a friend and I hitched from Italy to Germany to go to the Oktoberfest, only to realise that it had happened the week before.

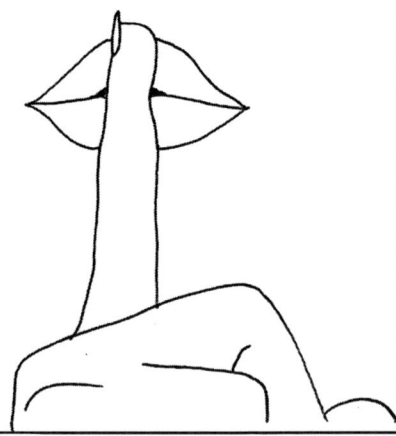

The Daring Mountain

"Which daring story shall I pick?" I asked myself while staring at the cursor on my computer, ready to type one of my amazing life stories.

I have never seen myself as a daring, courageous woman. I was rather shy when I was younger, often withdrawn and in my own little world.

However, if I look back with the judging eyes of my 47-year-old self today, I can certainly see so much courage and fearlessness in myself from a very young age.

* I remember hitchhiking all over Italy and Europe as a teenager, risking my safety many times. Like that time when I said to my parents that I was going camping with my friends only 50 km away from my home and ended up in Germany for the Oktoberfest. We even nearly slept on a bench in a park in Austria, only to be invited by lovely local people into their homes for a safer night.

* I left my country, Italy, at the age of 18 and adventured to London to live as an au pair.

* I travelled as a backpacker to more than 55 countries, often alone and doing very dangerous activities like swimming with dangerous animals, jumping off very high bridges or swimming underwater in dark caves not knowing if I would be able to swim back.

Certainly, all of this sounds very daring but nothing compares to the story I am going to tell you.

I am often so surprised when I see negative experiences we had in our childhood repeating themselves, as if we had not learnt anything.

I grew up in a very unhappy family. I still recall my mum and dad arguing all the time when my dad was choosing his beloved drinks and friends over my mum. It was chaos. It was drama on steroids. I do not remember seeing my mum very happy. Her happiness depended on my dad, on his behaviour, his mood and his response to her actions.

I secretly wished they separated because, somehow, they both looked very miserable. But they never did. My mum never had the courage to leave and go after what she truly loved.

My idea of love and what a relationship meant was very distorted. Love looked very painful, sacrificing. Love felt like a roller coaster of sadness and tiny happy moments stolen from a happily-ever-after book.

I was so naïve as a child, believing that love, for me, when I found it, would look completely different.

In fact, when I found it at the age of 23, all of the things I always hated and repelled about love were growing like weeds in my garden of love.

I spent the next six years feeling very miserable, unloved and not good enough. I was so aware of my unhappiness but somehow I could not run away from it. The pain and suffering became my addiction.

I used to spend days crying over endless arguments, fights, disrespect and cheating. I was cheated on a month before our marriage and I still went ahead with it, believing somehow that I could change this man and that I would live happily ever after like a heroine.

If I look at pictures of that time, I look so much older. You could see the pain in my eyes, the damage of the verbal abuse on my face, the smile that was gone forever.

Why was I doing this to myself? Leaving was not on the agenda and every day the light inside of me was dimming more and more.

That day, years later, still unhappy and miserable we decided to leave everything and go travelling for about a year in Central and South America.

"If your relationship is strong, it will survive, if not, it will be the end," someone told me before leaving.

You will have to wait until the end to see which turn my relationship took.

Travelling in so many different countries was incredible. We started in Mexico and ended up in Bolivia. So many adventures and interesting people on the way. But nothing seemed to put my heavy heart at peace. Somehow, I knew deep inside that the latter prediction from my friend was going to become true.

After separating for a few weeks while we were pursuing our adventures alone, I fell pregnant the night we reunited. I was in Costa Rica but I only found out weeks later while travelling in Colombia. I would never forget that test I took in the morning while in a hostel in Medellín. That moment marked the beginning of a very painful but liberating time of my life.

That same day something started to shift in me. All the yeses I had always said, the approval, the compromises – all collapsed like a sandcastle hit by a wave.

I remember sobbing like crazy when I broke the news. I have no idea where I found the courage to say, "No, I am keeping this baby, you can leave and do what you want, I am having this baby, alone."

I was ready to leave, to finally leave, to finally stop the sadness, and to stop repeating the story of my mother. I was not her, and it was time to take off that identity and find my own. I had so much rage inside.

How could have I allowed a man to treat me this badly, when I had seen my own dad doing the same to my mum? The humiliation I felt every time I looked at myself in the mirror was overwhelming, unbearable. The pain was like a sharp knife straight in my heart.

I kept travelling with my little one in my belly, I travelled through very dangerous roads, swimming in dangerous rivers, and one day, I even climbed a 5,000m mountain in Bolivia. I was the first to get to the top and I remember crying like a baby when I made that last step and stopped to look at the view.

I was touching my belly and I said to my little one, "We are going to make it, I promise you!"

The road to "make it" was a very painful road which took me back to London. At four months pregnant, I was sleeping on the floor at a friend's house, and looking for a job.

I was devastated, the saver in me wanted to save everything, his life, my life, our life, that of my child.

It took me a while to finally cut all the cords and live my life with my newborn child.

I often think that if it was not for him, I might not have survived the pain I felt.

Looking back at that moment now, I feel like a daring woman ...

I dared to leave my painful marriage, I dared to raise my child on my own, I dared to remarry again and believe in love. I dared to leave my secure 9–5 and start my own business doing what I love. I dared to invest money I did not have and take big risks. I dared to trust. I dared to share this story as a reminder that I am no longer the woman who says "yes" all the time. I dared to lock the hurt and victimised girl in the closet. I dared to believe in life again, in me, in my business.

And now, I am ready to dare to take other women up their own daring mountain and leave the mould and the old stories of their life behind, to reclaim a new, powerful, authentic, fearless identity.

We do not need to find ourselves, we are never LOST, we are inside of us, and there is a voice who is screaming there ...

Shhhhhh ... remain silent ... can you hear it?

YES, that one, do not pretend not to listen to it AGAIN. It is there, it has been suppressed for so long that it is used to being a whisper now. IT'S TIME YOU LISTENED TO IT.

I DID.

Start climbing your daring mountain.

Because your ego, your fears, will always stop you from shining in your life, and will blame everything else, like mine did, only to realise that it's you and only you who can change any given situations.

Dare now, whatever that might mean to you.

If not, the whispering voice will become mute soon and then what will become of you?

I listened, I did listen to that whisper that was there all along, that was telling me to leave, to let go, to stop repeating destructive patterns.

I dared to climb my own mountain, the way I desired, because I ultimately am the one to always lead myself.

Remember to always dare to desire, every day, every hour, every minute, every second, because ...
tomorrow is too late.

Debora Luzi

Grow and Reflect with Debora

Do you remember the game you probably used to play as a child? The one where you must choose to say the truth or dare to do something?

Truth or dare. Let's play it but we will add a twist, or better, we will take away a twist as we will only play dare, inviting truth, however, to be fully present.

I want you to stop for a moment and be fully present in the now. Let's leave the past or a moment ago behind, let's leave the future or tomorrow for tomorrow's thoughts and connect to your heart. Put a hand on it and close your eyes.

Can you feel the beat of your heart? Can you feel its burning desires? Can you feel how alive it is?

Breathe deeply and slowly. Now listen to the whisper of your heart. Is there anything it wants to tell you? Is there anything it is dying for you to do, to follow, to dare to pursue?

Take a moment to connect. Do not overthink this moment, allow yourself to be transported by the spontaneity of this moment, by the spontaneity of your thoughts and desires.

Take a moment to notice the possible uncomfortable feelings which are rising in your body and taking over your mind. Maybe some of your heart desires are making you fearful, doubtful and shameful.

Allow your body to feel and stay with any feelings that might come up for you.

There are no right or wrong feelings, only the in-the-moment feelings which we must honour and welcome.

Now grab a pen and start writing. I will guide you with the questions below to feel the daring passion of your heart.

1. What is your heart truly desiring to do? Is there something that you might regret not doing or saying if you were to leave this earth tomorrow? It might be even the smallest thing, something you have been avoiding thinking about it for fear of being wrong or not appropriate.

   Journal here on whatever comes up for you.

2. What are the fears rising when you think about daring to take that action, do the thing your heart is telling you to do? Be honest and go deep within yourself to find the reason behind the fears.

   Once you find each fear, explore it, analyse it and question if the opposite could be also true.

3. I now DARE you to take any action right now, even the smallest one, to listen to your heart whisper, to follow that desire that longs to be listened to. If you knew all will be well, what action would you take right now?

CONTACT DEBORA

 www.facebook.com/debora.luzi.9

 www.instagram.com/deboraluziofficial/

 www.deboraluzi.com

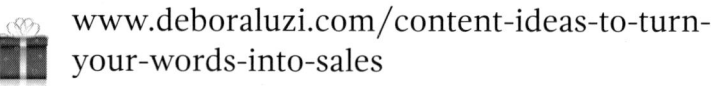 www.deboraluzi.com/content-ideas-to-turn-your-words-into-sales

Space for your thoughts ...

....
....
....
....
....
....
....
....
....
....
....
....
....
....
....
....
....
....
....

DRAW THE DARING WOMAN IN YOU

We hope you have enjoyed this journey together.

We are confident that you have discovered many parts of yourself you did not remember existed.

We would love you to remember this moment and the shifts and breakthroughs you might have had while reading.

To help you remember them and take them with you into your daily life we have dedicated the next activity to your realisations and the new version of you that might have risen.

Let's mark it. Let's draw it.

Let's leave a footprint of it on this book and in your life.

Grab a pen and colours, draw the outline of your body, and draw the daring woman you are. Add words, features, characteristics, and strengths you might have discovered about yourself after reading our beautiful stories.

Write about your desires and who you are.

Let your creative side steal the show.

NOW it's time to write your story

Writing it will not only give you a sense of freedom but a knowing that someone out there is ready to listen to it ...

Because their life is about to change because of it.

Before you do, I would love to help you tap into the hidden feelings and words that might need to get out right now.

I have created a beautiful meditation that will help you tap into your intuition and heart and write in total flow as if no one is watching as if the only person who matters is YOU.

◈ Before we start please go and grab a pen and hold it on your right hand

◈ Sit comfortably in a quiet place. Make sure you will not be distracted for at least 10 minutes

◈ Gently close your eyes and take three big breaths

◈ Breathe in and breathe out

◈ As you breathe in and out focus your attention in the now. You are here, sitting down, your body touching the floor or the chair. You can hear noises from outside. You can hear the noise of your own mind

◈ There is no yesterday, not a moment or an hour ago. There is no tomorrow, or later. All there is, is NOW. Right here in this exact moment

◈ Become aware of what is around you and what is in you

◈ Now focus your attention into the middle of your eyes, in the third eye chakra (chakra is a centre of energy in our body, which means 'wheels' in Sanskrit). Hold a pen in your right hand and put it into this point and start spinning your hand clockwise, making small circles

◈ As you spin, imagine a strong purple light entering this area, and as you spin imagine hearing your intuition speaking to you. Your intuition is the voice of your higher self, which knows exactly what is best for you in your life. The voice that is not subject to limitations or conditionings, the voice of your soul

◈ Carefully listen to those voices or whispers. As your hand spins, you hear the voices, the whispers get louder and clearer

◈ What are they telling you? Are they giving you ideas, thoughts, actions to take?

◈ Let them flow into you with no judgement

◈ As you keep spinning your hand in circles, you hear more and more whispers. You are ready to listen

◈ Now repeat out loud or in your mind, "Thank you, I am ready to listen, I am ready to allow my intuition to speak to me and guide me, and so it is, and so it is, and so it is."

◈ Now gently move your hand to your heart area. Start spinning your hand clockwise and make small circles. As you spin your hand imagine connecting to your heart. Hear its beat, "tu tum. Tu tum," imagine you and your heart becoming one

💎 With each spin hear your heart speaking to you. Be open to listening to it. What does your heart want to tell you? What are your heart's desires? What are the feelings and emotions that your heart feels right now? What are the feelings and emotions, the stories that your heart secretly hides?

💎 Be ready to listen

💎 Remain silent for a few minutes and simply listen and feel

💎 Connect to every single emotion stored in your heart, even the ones you might feel ashamed of. The secret ones, the ones you are trying to forget and hide. There cannot be shame in your heart as every emotion you felt or are still feeling is part of your journey and made you who you are today. Own your journey, your story and all the emotions and memories attached to it. Know deep in your heart that gold can be found in all the scars you carry

💎 Now repeat out loud or in your mind, "I am ready to listen to you, I am ready to feel, and I am ready to be, and so it is and so it is and so it is."

💎 Feel the warmth of your heart in your hand and feel this beautiful connection between you and your heart

💎 Now put your left hand into your third eye and your right hand to your heart and slowly bring them together into your mouth (the area of your throat chakras, where your real voice comes from, where your truth is spoken)

◈ Imagine the whispers from your third eye and the desires and the feelings from your heart all joining together into the mouth or throat chakra area, ready to be freed and expressed.

◈ Open your mouth wide and make a strong and firm "ahhhh" sound, letting all these words come out of you, ready to be expressed and ready to be written onto paper

◈ Get them all out, sound "ahhhhhh" a few times until all the words have imaginably come out

◈ Take three deep breaths, put your feet firm on the ground to ground yourself and gently open your eyes

You are ready to write your truth now.

You are ready to write with your true voice, no more excuses.

I have recorded this meditation for you so that you can listen to it anytime you need some writing inspiration.

You can download it from this link:
www.deboraluzi.com/meditation

Let's bring your story to life ...

Now, go and grab a photo of you and add it here. If you do not have one, it might be time to take a new one, even if simply with your phone. Remember to act as the daring woman you are and maybe add features to the photo you have discovered about yourself. You may want to look fiercer, and more passionate; you may want to smile. You may want to put that red lipstick on or the hat you always desired to wear. Dare! Because now you are a woman who dares to desire. It's time to write your story, and remember that the world is your stage and the WORD is YOUR OYSTER!

(Title)

By

(Your name)

MY STORY

_____

_____

_____

_____

_____

_____

_____

_____

_____

_____

_____

_____

_____

_____

_____

_____

_____

_____

_____

_____

_____

_____

_____

_____

_____

_____

_____

_____

_____

_____

_____

_____

_____

_____

_____

_____

_____

_____

Women Who Dare To Desire

How do you feel about sharing your story?

In whatever form you like.

You may want to publish it, or start telling it on stages all over the world ...

The word and your story are your oysters.

Remember your story is your GOLD and your scars are portals to the deepest, purest version of yourself, who has always been alive and present.

You just need to remember WHO SHE IS!

ACKNOWLEDGEMENTS FROM ALL OF THE AUTHORS.

Debora Luzi would like to thank all the beautiful co-authors in this book for trusting the vision she had for this book.

A special thanks to all the women who will read this book and trust that something is ready to be shifted in their lives.

Elisa Colangeli would like to acknowledge her husband Felice and her sons, Giacomo and Daniele. Every single day they give her the opportunity to experience love and support in her little family nest.

Tina Eloise would like to thank all those outspoken, paradigm-shifting women that have come before her for paving the way and showing her how.

All those women that stand alongside her for supporting & inspiring her. She would like to thank all those women that will come after her for giving her purpose and hope.

Gaia Sciaranghella would like to thank Debora Luzi and the book co-authors for the wonderful opportunity to reach all the readers. She is as well grateful to all the women who will read this book and trust it as a guide for their own journey, and finally to her family for their continuous support.

Sara Annes Matos would like to thank Debora Luzi for creating the space for unravelling this message and her friends Gary Pollard and Ann Harikeertan for their unconditional support. And finally, Sara would like to thank her Soul and all the parts of her that show up every day to do this thing called life!

Dorothy Watt would like to thank all the homoeopaths who have supported her on her journey to date, especially the homoeopathic GP who started it all. Each of them has helped her think further, higher, deeper and wider outside the box!

Julie Shapiro would like to acknowledge Debora Luzi and her amazing community of talented healers, coaches, artists and writers in the Writing Academy. Through this community, Julie has rediscovered her creativity and joy. She is grateful to Debora and the Writing Academy members for all of the amazing lessons, the wild inspiration, and the loving support and encouragement they have shared with her.

She also would like to thank Eileen Savel, her dear friend and "the best editor ever." Eileen, Julie appreciates your attention and dedication to her work. And last, but not least, Julie sends gratitude and love to her late mother, Dorothy Shapiro for inspiring her creative spirit.

Lucia Margarida Pestana would like to thank Debora Luzi for holding her hand and everyone who was present on this journey. She would also like to thank her inner child for being her strength!

Loredana Thoenig is grateful for being part of this amazing group of daring women who collaborated on this book. She would like to thank Debora for bringing them together and giving her the opportunity to share part of her wisdom. She dedicates this book to her amazing children who want to see her always shine. And to all the women who will read and be inspired by this book.

Made in United States
North Haven, CT
31 March 2023

34821704R00104